BEYOND THE

BEYOND THE FINAL FRONTIER

Near Death Experiences and the Afterlife

DR RICHARD KENT WITH DAVID WAITE

Marshall Pickering
An Imprint of HarperCollins*Publishers*

Marshall Pickering is an imprint of
HarperCollins*Religious*
part of HarperCollins*Publishers*
77-85 Fulham Palace Road, London W6 8JB
www.christian-publishing.com

First published in Great Britain in 2000
by Marshall Pickering

3 5 7 9 10 8 6 4 2

A catalogue record for this book
is available from the British Library.

ISBN 0 551 03203 0

Printed and bound in Great Britain by
Omnia Books Limited, Glasgow

CONTENTS

ABOUT THE AUTHORS AND THE FINAL FRONTIER WEBSITE

Dr Richard Kent

Dr Richard Kent is a retired General Practitioner, aged 53. His first book, *The Final Frontier*, (co-authored with Val Fotherby), has been well received, and has also been translated into German and Italian. He qualified at the age of 22, and settled in General Practice at the age of 27. He is happily married and has three daughters.

Richard and his wife became Christians in 1974. Richard was at the time seeking for a deeper meaning to life. He had already tried various avenues such as sport and charitable pursuits, before he finally became a Christian. Richard and his wife are trustees of The Final Frontier Charitable Trust. Richard also runs marathons for various charities.

Richard is a speaker for the Full Gospel Business Men's Fellowship International, usually on the subject of life after death, although he occasionally speaks on Creation, scientific evidence for the Bible, end-time prophecy and Bible numerics. To contact Richard for speaking engagements, or for any purpose, please write to him or e-mail him at the following address:

Dr Richard Kent
Full Gospel Business Men's Fellowship International
UK Field Office
PO Box 11
Knutsford
Cheshire WA16 6QP
United Kingdom

Tel: 01565 632667
Fax: 01565 755639
E-mail: drrkent@aol.com

The Final Frontier Website

This website is a growing database of Christian Near Death Experiences, Bible study, and relevant Christian research. A further book, *Return from the Final Frontier*, will be written when we have received sufficient Near Death Experience stories. Please e-mail or write to Dr Richard Kent if you have a Near Death Experience to relate, at the above address. The website may be accessed at the following address: www.finalfrontier.org.uk

The Final Frontier Charitable Trust

The Final Frontier Charitable Trust is a Christian charity which promotes the Gospel of Jesus Christ, and makes donations to various Christian charities and ministries, both in the UK and abroad.

David Waite

David Waite was born in Cheshire in 1946, and lived there, working in Local Government, until the early 1970s when he moved to Oxfordshire in order to join a missionary organization. He became a Christian when he was 18, at a Christian holiday week held at Filey in Yorkshire.

He has been writing since 1988. His best selling autobiography, entitled *One Step at a Time*, was published by Kingsway in 1989. After the book was published he began to write for a number of Christian magazines and newspapers in the United Kingdom, and has interviewed a wide range of Christians in the show business and sports world, as well as full-time Christian workers in the United Kingdom and abroad.

In 1998 he worked on a book with Sheila Barlow, who had been part of Saddam Hussein's human shield during the Gulf War. This book, *Stepping Through My Nightmares*, won the prestigious Christian Broadcasting Council's Gold Award for the Best Non-Fiction Christian Book of 1998.

David has been married for 26 years and has four children. He and his wife live in a town on the edge of the Cotswolds. David has been a frequent after dinner speaker at FGBMFI and church meetings in Britain, as well as occasionally broadcasting on local radio in the 'Thought for the Day' slot.

To contact David for speaking engagements, writing, broadcasting, or any other purpose, please write to him, or e-mail him, at the following address:

David Waite
Full Gospel Business Men's Fellowship International
UK Field Office
PO Box 11
Knutsford
Cheshire WA16 6QP
United Kingdom

Tel: 01565 632667
Fax: 01565 755639
E-mail: davidwaite-witney@freecall-uk.co.uk

Note from the Authors

The purpose of this book is simply to present the reality of eternal life to the reader in an interesting and exciting format.

Following the success of *The Final Frontier*, published by HarperCollins in 1997, this new book contains more stories of near death experiences. However, more space is devoted in this second book to establishing the reality of God, the fact the Bible is totally supernatural, and a deeper study of life after death, according to the Bible.

ACKNOWLEDGEMENTS

The authors are most grateful to Dr John Sloan, Consultant in Accident and Emergency at Leeds General Infirmary, for his most helpful introduction to the book, and also for his chapter, 'Why I believe in the Resurrection.'

The authors are extremely grateful to Chuck Missler of Koinonia House, USA, for his kind permission to quote facts and figures from his excellent audiocassette briefing packages, in particular *The Creator Beyond Time and Space*. The authors gratefully acknowledge Chuck Missler's research, and the appropriate briefing package details are quoted in each case. Chuck Missler's ministry address and website details are quoted under 'Other Information' at the end of this book.

The stories of Dr Terry Elder and Buddy Farris are reproduced from *Voice*, the official magazine of the Full Gospel Business Men's Fellowship International, and are included with their kind permission.

The testimony of Rev. Kenneth Hagin is reproduced with kind permission from Kenneth Hagin Ministries, of which details are given with his story.

The testimony of Rev. Mickey Robinson is reproduced with kind permission from Mickey Robinson Ministries, of which details are given with his story.

The story of Rev. Howard Pittman is excerpted from his booklet, *Placebo*, and reprinted with his kind permission. Details of Rev. Howard Pittman's ministry are given with his story.

The extract from Bill W. by Robert Thomsen, published by Perennial Library, 1975, is used with permission.

Vicki's story is taken from *Mindsight: Near-Death and Out-of-Body Experiences in the Blind* by Kenneth Ring and Sharon Cooper (William James Center for Consciousness Studies, 1999) and used by permission.

The authors would like to acknowledge Kevin Williams' excellent web site, *Near Death Experiences and the Afterlife*, and thank him for his kind permission to reproduce stories from his web site. In each case the correct Internet web site address of the story has been given.

The authors would also like to acknowledge Jerry Senear's excellent web site, *Christian Near-Death Experiences*, and to thank him for his kind permission to reproduce stories from his web site. In each case the correct Internet web site address of the story has been given.

The authors would like to thank Seattle IANDS for their kind permission to reproduce Lorraine Tutmarc's story. Details of Seattle IANDS are given with the story.

A number of other individuals have kindly consented for their stories to be included in this book, and the authors are extremely grateful to every single contributor.

INTRODUCTION

by Dr John Sloan FRCS, FFAEM, Consultant in Accident & Emergency, Leeds General Infirmary, UK

I have spent many hours of my professional life resuscitating patients following cardiac arrest or severe trauma. With the passage of time, I realize more and more that this is an enormous privilege for medical, nursing and paramedical staff. It is difficult to communicate the joy of knowing that you have just brought a fellow human being back from certain death.

Resuscitation, unfortunately, still ends in death in many instances. I have been aware in such cases that the precious spirit within my patient is leaving their body. And at that moment there is nothing medical science can do to reverse it. But what is really happening in these critical moments? Who has the authority or knowledge to say?

At this time, perhaps more than at any other, there is massive and increasing interest in the supernatural. Near-death experiences have been recorded for many years, and entire belief systems have been built around them. So a book about real accounts of near-death experiences may simply encourage such interest. To do this is risky, to say the least, and could be compared to constructing a religion based around ghosts or UFOs. This was not Richard Kent's intention in his first book, *The Final Frontier*. It is certainly not our intention in this follow-up book, which is why we have included sections on the supernatural authority of the Bible, and what the Bible clearly teaches about life after death. Near-death experiences need to be interpreted in the light of what we already know from the Bible. We are greatly indebted to the help of Chuck Missler, who has international standing in his field. He has given us permission to quote his material, to help us establish both the existence of God and the supernatural origin of the Bible.

In the history of human civilization no one has had such convincing knowledge of life after death as Jesus Christ. I use the word 'convincing' because He predicted what would happen, then carried it out. In fact before He was born many details of His life were foretold in 332 Old Testament prophecies. Sceptics would say that He simply chose to live these out, but many of the prophecies include details about which He had no choice, humanly speaking. Such prophecies include where He would be born, who His ancestry would be, who His mother would be, and who would visit Him as a baby. Chuck Missler has calculated that the chance of one man fulfilling 48 of the key prophecies is a staggering $1:10^{157}$.

To most of us this does not mean very much. However, if I were to mark a single atom and hide it somewhere in the universe, and then ask someone to select one atom at random, then the chance of that person finding my marked atom would be $1:10^{66}$. If I then asked the same person to make a new choice every second for a billion years, the chance of that person finding my marked atom would be $1:10^{83}$, which is infinitely less likely than one person fulfilling 48 prophecies, by $1:10^{74}$.

Returning to something we can grasp, perhaps the most stunning fact from Jesus' life is that He said that He would be killed and would rise again from the dead. This is exactly what He did. Having risen from the dead He was seen by 500 people. Bearing in mind that most of those people were still alive when the written claim was made, common legal practice dictates that this statement was, and is, true. If one bears in mind that to proclaim the fact publicly caused nearly all the New Testament writers to be executed, legal practice again confirms the truth of their statement concerning the truth of the resurrection of Jesus Christ.

To my mind these facts give Jesus Christ a credibility which is unrivalled. I believe what He said. I believe He was God in human form. Moreover, the Bible asserts that Jesus Christ was present, with God the Father, and God the Holy Spirit, before anything was created, that all things were made by Him, and that the entire physical world is held together by Him!

It would take some time to elaborate on this statement, but the Bible states: 'By Him all things were created: things in Heaven and on Earth, visible and invisible, whether thrones or powers or rulers or authorities; all things were created by Him and for Him' (Colossians 1:16, 17).

In the Bible the life and wisdom of Jesus Christ are clearly stated in John 1:1 and 14, where the term 'the Word' is used to describe Jesus Christ: 'In the beginning was the Word, and the Word was with God, and the Word was God. The Word became flesh and made His dwelling among us ... We have seen His glory, the glory of the one and only, who came from the Father, full of grace and truth.'

This states that Jesus Christ is God in human form who has gone before us. He was the author of life itself, and communicates His life and wisdom in the Bible. We would therefore be well advised to take seriously what Jesus Christ actually said. The makeup of mankind is portrayed in the Bible, and it is not surprising that clues are given about the near-death experience.

Over the years Christian writers have drawn a distinction between the body, the soul and the spirit. While the nature of the soul and the spirit is misunderstood in current expression, and even used interchangeably, the Bible is clear about the distinction. The soul is the mix of mind, emotions and will, that make up the human character. The spirit is deep within, and is the site of our conscience. The spirit is the unique place where God can be known. The spirit lives on after the death of the body.

Since the spirit lives on after death, it follows that the spirit is separated from the body at death. It follows, too, that the spirit may well meet the Author of life itself. Exactly what happens at this astonishing meeting is for each of us to discover when we die. A few, however, may have been privileged to make this discovery ahead of time.

This is the context in which this book is written. Read this book, be stimulated by it, and let it point you to the One who gives all life and light, Jesus Christ.

2 MICKEY ROBINSON

Parachute jumping was Mickey Robinson's passion – until the night when everything started to go wrong, and he found himself ablaze from head to foot. Everyone said that he would die – but they reckoned without God.

It was just another hot August night to the four men and myself who were all set to make a routine parachute jump. Flying conditions were poor, due to the combination of intense heat and high humidity. I wasn't concerned, though, I was a professional skydiver and had worked in a demonstration team before crowds of thousands. Not all in the plane were as relaxed as I was. It was one man's first jump; for another it was only his fourth. Skydiving was my life – nothing else mattered. It had won my heart since I witnessed a display by a parachuting school. The progression, from my first jump to my first free-fall, was rapid. I was obsessed – no amount of time or money was too much to spend. Eventually I was jumping with some of the world's best skydivers.

I would witness to people in bars, trying to convert them to my passion ... I even had bumper stickers. Old friends were concerned that I was going overboard, but I didn't care. I was 100 per cent committed to skydiving, and knew I was in complete control of my life. That night, with a full load of six, the plane cleared the runway, going well over 100 miles per hour. Suddenly, without any warning, the engines totally failed. The pilot turned to me and said, 'We're going down!' The plane plunged towards the Earth, and impacted where the wing joined the fuselage. It then spun, cartwheeling over the wings, and I slammed into the ground. I was flung forward, smacking my face against the hard interior wall. Injured and in shock, three skydivers escaped the wreckage and ran. A fourth also exited. He saw the pilot and myself moving and assumed that we were escaping also. As he left, the plane burst into flames – the fuel tank had ruptured and, as the plane spun, gasoline splashed everywhere. Terrified, he bolted, screaming, and suddenly realized that we were still inside the plane. Running back into the flaming wreckage, he saw me, aflame from head to toe, trying to free my leg which was trapped in a hole where the wing had been. He yelled for the pilot to unbuckle, and attempted to pull me loose. But I was stuck!

I was born in 1949 in Cleveland, Ohio, during the 'happy days' era, and I grew up with attitudes reflecting the mood of the society. I lived for the things I desired, and life was something that wasn't meant to be taken seriously. I went to church every Sunday (my family were Roman Catholics), so I was endowed with a knowledge of God. However, I had never encountered anyone who knew Him personally.

As I grew older, I began to entertain concepts other than Biblical ones, relating to the universe, creation and eternity. I turned away the simplicity of the gospel which had been a relevant factor in my life (though I had never been converted), and became involved in the usual teenage lifestyle of dating and sports.

After graduating from high school, I talked my way into a job in a stockbroker's firm. By then I thought I was a big shot and really had it together! People were amazed at what I had accomplished.

At 18 years of age I was really going places. I worked in downtown Cleveland in a modern, progressive office surrounded with many attractive people: my job was fun, very challenging and exciting.

Outwardly I was a confident, attractive young man – the life of the party. Inwardly, though, I was driven by fear – fear of not measuring up, of failing. I was always seeking the approval of other people. Though I appeared to have it all together, I was actually living on the very edge of desperation.

Now I was desperate! Ablaze from head to toe, and trapped in the wreckage, unable to wrench myself free! My rescuer's second attempt succeeded as, with greater than human strength, he pulled so hard he tore me loose. Dragging me from the plane, he threw me on the ground and rolled me around to put the fire out. It took several attempts as the fire kept reigniting. When finally he'd stopped the flames, he turned back for the pilot but it was too late. The pilot had been burnt to death.

I lay on the ground, severely injured. The skin on my arm and hand was falling off on to the ground like that of a fried chicken. There was also a serious cut on my face. I asked how badly I was burned and the comment was, with all the smoke, they could not tell. Actually, they were convinced that I would never make it off the field. When the medics cut off what remained of my clothing, they saw that I had sustained very serious third-degree burns over a third of my body.

Although I was young, extremely healthy and very athletic, the prognosis was bad: I had no chance of survival, especially as burns to the extent that I had received often lead to severe complications – and they did.

In the days and weeks that followed, my entire body became infected, and I dropped in weight from 167 pounds of solid muscle to 90 pounds. My body became thin and wasted, and open sores developed that exposed my very bones. The back of my heels rotted away and my hand was so badly infected they expected to amputate it.

I was in tremendous pain. There were excruciating external ulcers and an internal ulcer from the over-secretion of gastric juices that burned a hole in my stomach. This caused a lot of internal bleeding. A third of my oesophagus was destroyed and it scarred together so that I could not even drink water. My blood was infested with micro-organisms and there were days when I had fluid loss of as much as 10 pints – almost the entire volume of the human body. I also had a head injury and a contusion of my brain.

My body was fighting as hard as it could against death, but it was a losing battle. Each one of my complications was enough to kill a person. I was blind in my right eye. As time went on my body became rigid, and the nerves in both my legs died. My muscles became flaccid, and my feet curled up like withered claws over the end of the bed.

The doctors had done all they could – given me medicine, cleansed my sores and treated me in every way they knew how. They even called in an expert from a university hospital. Several years later I read the summary of his medical examination.

Part of the time I was unconscious, and there was no visible response. There were other times when I was as alert as I am now. Often, I was somewhere between these two states. Most of all I remember being very sick and could actually feel my life draining out of me like someone throwing switches in a switch box.

As I lay dying, my temperature reached a high of 106 degrees. I was so uncomfortable that if someone laid even their hand on the bed, I would cringe with suffering. My whole body was racked with agony, every cell stressed out; yet as I lay there I could sense that my body was still fighting to survive.

During this time I had a life-changing experience. In an instant the physical world vanished and my inner man came out of my physical body. I was no longer in the hospital room – I had entered into the realm of the spirit. Immediately I became aware of two things: that the spiritual world is the real world, and the absence of the sensory perception of time.

It was awesome! I found myself travelling somewhere and had no control over this.

Suddenly, there appeared to be a doorway closing. A great darkness began to surround me, and I saw this was actually a point of separation. Coming through the closing space was a beam of the purest, whitest light I had ever seen. The doorway began closing faster and faster. The meaning of this separation became illuminated to me. I knew that if this door closed completely, I would be cut off for all eternity from this light.

I experienced a deep hopelessness and horror. Separation is hopelessness! External separation is a torment beyond belief. I want you to know there is a place established somewhere that is eternal separation. I was permitted not only to see, but to experience the feeling of what it would be like to be in this eternal separation. And I began to cry out to God.

I have been asked, 'Were you a Christian when this happened?' The night they brought me into the emergency room, although I do not remember, I asked my mother to send for a priest I had known in the past. He came quickly to my side, anointed me with oil and prayed for me.

A repentance process began at this time. As I was lying there, very injured, sick unto death, I cried out, 'God, I'm sorry! Please give me another chance!' Many times I went through the swinging doors into surgery, not knowing if I would wake up, and this knowledge started something inside me. I did not know how to pray, but I begged God for forgiveness.

As I stood on the very edge of eternity with this door closing and the darkness beginning to envelop me, I knew that in one second I could be separated for eternity from the Source of all life! And I began to scream out the same things as I had prayed when I was awake, 'God, I want to live! I'm sorry! Please give me another chance!'

The grace and the mercy of God is beyond our comprehension! Instantly I was caught up into Heaven; what a contrast! Eternal love and comfort compared to eternal hopelessness. I knew now I would never die. I had a deep awareness of eternal life – and was assured absolutely that I would always be comforted and cared for. The Bible says, 'in His presence is the fullness of joy and at His right hand are pleasures for ever more' (Psalm 16:11). The glory and power of God was everywhere over me, under me, around me, vibrating through me.

Then the Lord began to reveal to me future events. I saw seconds, days, weeks, months and years go by in front of me – all connected together. I did not see just one day here and there and skip to another. I saw time – I do not know how God does this, but He has the ability. I saw myself seeing people I never knew as if I did know them; it was as if I was watching something on television. Some of the events were greatly magnified in my vision: then I would go on to something else, at times I saw myself doing some dumb things that I should not be doing and wanted to call out to myself, 'Don't do that!' But I had to just watch, and then the scene would go on to something else.

The Lord told me that I was coming back to Earth. He did not speak in a language like I'm using now, but the knowledge and awareness that I was being sent back just came to me. Immediately, as if someone had strings and was reeling me in like a kite, I began to travel back to the life I had come from. As I settled into my physical body, I could actually feel my spirit pressing through my flesh. Can you imagine what it would feel like to have the wind blowing through the leaves of a tree? This, as I imagine it, is similar to what I experienced at that time as my spirit meshed into my flesh. Suddenly, I could see again out of my physical eyes and hear out of my physical ears.

As I began to return to normal consciousness, I realized that I was speaking in a beautiful language, and wondered what was happening. As soon as I had this thought the language stopped, and I became aware that I was alive. The temperature of 106 degrees was broken, and I fell into a natural sleep for the first time since the injury. When I woke up several hours later I was sticking painfully to the sheets from the blood and sweat, but was resting in a sea of peace! For the first time in my life, I knew what true peace was.

As the days went by my condition continued to improve, although the nerves in both my legs were still dead.

The next year was spent almost continuously in the hospital, followed by a further four years in and out of medical institutions. It was a very long haul! I had between 75 and 100 operations. People did the best they could to take care of me.

I did not understand what had happened to me spiritually. I was saved, born again and filled with the Spirit, yet unaware of what these things meant. There was nothing in my previous experience or understanding to help me relate to what was happening to me spiritually.

I began to heal, slowly at first. One leg began to return to usefulness; the other remained unresponsive. The nerve that ran down the front of my leg was quite dead; it would not respond when tests of electrical impulses were applied to it. The muscle was totally flaccid and the foot hung down – I could not move it. They fitted me with a leg brace.

After nearly a year, this leg was instantly healed – it was marvellous! I had begun speaking to my legs every day saying, 'Legs go!' and though the right leg was obedient, the left leg was continually rebellious. It never submitted to my command. Then one day as I did this, my left foot popped up, and I was walking

– it was quite an experience! I took off my leg brace and threw it away, never to touch it again.

I have had many marvellous healings. Around five years after the accident, sight was restored in my blind eye, after a surgical procedure.

Today I enjoy life! I play with my children, run, snow ski and ride horses. This is marvellous considering I was never expected to walk again. It is incredible to have this lifestyle now, when there was so much taken away.

Due to my burn injuries I'm a pretty funny looking guy now, but by the grace of God I am still relatively unselfconscious, amazingly for someone who's been so vain.

I'd like to take this opportunity to note how there is a natural tendency, even among Christians, to function in our own strength. I know what it's like – that's how I used to live before my accident. But now I know what it's like to be weak, totally bankrupt of strength and devoid of any possibility of helping myself. There was no help in this world for me. There was not a doctor that could fix me: my loved ones could do nothing. However there were relatives who'd never met me, who were supernaturally led to pray for me. The strength of God was poured through their intercessory hearts and, through the power of God, death was defeated!

I would not recommend my experience to anyone, yet it taught me the utter importance of living by God's strength. We all need to make the conscious decision to stop relying on our own abilities and to live by the strength of God.

For further information, and teaching material, please contact:

Rev Mickey Robinson
PO Box 682485
Franklin
TN 37608-2485
USA

Fax: 001-615-790-1267
Web site: www.mickeyrobinson.com

3 JENNIFER REES LARCOMBE

One thing that mums are good at is keeping well. With a family to look after and a house to run, any ailments that they may encounter get quickly put to one side, in the hope that they will go away. And most times they do. But the aches and pains that Jennifer Rees Larcombe did her best to ignore put her into hospital and brought her close to death. Jennifer's fascinating story is told in full in her book Unexpected Healing, *published by Hodder and Stoughton.*

Before I started to feel ill it seemed as though I had everything that I could wish for. A loving husband, six adorable children, a wonderful house in the country and good friends. I used to daydream as a child about the life I wanted to have when I grew up. All the things I had at that point in time were on the list, as well as a collection of animals, which I also enjoyed. In my childish daydreams even a goat had been somewhere on the list, and although I never acquired one of those, we had ducks instead.

One of our six children had not been born to me and my husband Tony. Jane was the daughter of friends, who had both tragically died. She was only three when her mum died of cancer, and then her dad died of a heart attack some four years later. When she was brought to us by the social worker the afternoon she had discovered her father's body outside his bed-room door, Jane still had no idea that he was dead. When Tony told her she said, 'Well, that's all right – I'll come and stay with you then.' In spite of her confident statement, Jane was in fact very concerned about my health particularly, and used to cling on to me if I so much as sneezed! Very often she would say, 'You're not going to die, are you?' and I would reassure her that I was fit and well, and would probably live to be a hundred.

So when I felt the first signs of illness, I brushed them off as nothing to be concerned about. I had to keep well, if only to keep my promise to Jane. And in fact, one by one, the symptoms I started to experience were nothing to worry about. A bout of flu that wouldn't go away, a feeling of tiredness that persisted, limbs that felt as heavy as lead. Then I had to admit that the headache that had been with me for ages, was just not moving. I started to swallow vitamin pills like Smarties, and go on long walks around the countryside that I lived in, determined to keep fit and get the better of my maladies. But things went from bad to worse. I began to fall over, due to the dizzy spells that came upon me with increased frequency. To my relief, the children thought it a huge joke, but I swore them to secrecy as far as Tony was concerned. I didn't want him carting me off to the doctor. I felt that if doctors got involved, it would start to get out of my control.

It was one morning while I was doing something as mun-dane as cleaning the bath that I realized I was in need of some medical help. I had an acute headache, and my neck was com-pletely stiff. I was seeing four bath taps instead of two, and then I realized I could not make my arm bend or my hand grip the sponge. My whole body started to feel out of control, and I thought I was going mad.

Our GP examined me the next morning, and in a short space of time he was phoning for an ambulance to take me to our local hospital, suspecting me of having encephalitis, an acute inflammation of the brain. After I was taken to a ward all I wanted to do was sleep, but every so often I would be stirred from my slumbers by nurses or doctors who needed to do tests. By now, even my speech was slurred, and I worried that people who didn't know any better might think I had been taking drugs, but after a while I ceased to worry even about that. They had placed me in a small room off the main ward, away from the noise that was generated there. Cot sides were put around my bed. I am very fond of animals, and in my confused state, I thought that it might be to keep the goats out! My legs had grown so heavy that I thought at times there might be a goat sitting on my bed.

People came and went over the next week, and I remained in a semi-conscious state. I was told that I would be moved to another hospital the next day, and wondered in my jumbled mind how I would manage the journey on my own.

Then I had a visit from my minister, Brian, and his wife. I was reassured by their presence, and felt everything was going to be all right. I mumbled something about going to Heaven, and Brian said that he understood what I was saying but he was going to pray for me anyway. I still remember his lovely warm voice just melting away, and thinking at the same time that it was too much of an effort to breathe, and realizing it was far easier not to bother.

Then, at the foot of my bed, I was suddenly aware of a light beginning to glow. As I looked, it grew brighter. I was curious. Light of any kind had been painful for some time, but this one didn't hurt my eyes. It seemed to have magnetic qualities about it, and, sure enough, I felt drawn towards it. Then I was aware of what seemed to be a cave opening up in the darkness of the wall, leading upwards and out of the room. I felt myself floating effortlessly away from my body. I found that moving my arms and legs was no longer painful, and in fact I could do cartwheels if I wanted to! I presumed that it must feel like this when one is falling from an aeroplane, except that I was going up, not down! 'So this is what dying feels like,' I thought. 'If I had known it was like this I wouldn't have worried. At the end of the tunnel I'm going to meet God at long last.'

I sensed that I was standing on the threshold of somewhere far more wonderful and beautiful than I had ever encountered, and below was the darkness and pain that I had left behind. I had had a relationship with God since I was a small child, and I felt His presence waiting there for me, although I did not see Him. What I did see were lights – thousands of coloured lights, in every shade imaginable, all indescribably lovely, glowing soft like rainbows. Think of a colour and it was there – turquoise, pink, yellow and blue, and in one heavenly kaleidoscope.

I knew at this point that I had a choice – I could press on to where I would meet my Maker, and be with Him forever, or I could return to the world, and all the problems and difficulties I faced. The choice was mine. I hated making decisions at the best of times, but everything seemed to be waiting for me to do so. Then I thought of Tony and the children, and with a strange feeling of disappointment, I decided to return, a decision I have often regretted since.

As I returned to my body, deep in my spirit I heard the Lord speaking to me. 'From this moment you will begin to recover and go back. It's going to be a struggle, but I will give you My strength,' He said.

I felt the pain return as I re-entered my body. Brian was still praying for me, but he quickly brought things to a close, as the nurses started to buzz around me. I did start to feel better, almost immediately. I spent the night remembering those amazing colours and what had happened to me, but the sense of anti-climax was devastating. With my ability to think more clearly came the realization that I was seriously ill. And although I did have to spend several years in a wheelchair, I was eventually completely healed and now enjoy good health again.

I used to have a real fear of death – not of actually being dead, but the dying process, and now that has totally gone. Looking back I suppose death was the thing I feared the most, and now I know that there is absolutely nothing to fear at all.

4 BUDDY FARRIS

Policemen are trained to deal with every eventuality. But nothing could have prepared Buddy Farris for what was to happen to him after he apprehended a speeding car on a busy highway one Thanksgiving Eve in the USA.

Engrossed in my book, at first I failed to notice the speeders multiplying on this dark Thanksgiving Eve. The radar ticked off the count ... 60, 65, 70, 75, 80.

When another flashed by at 82, I set the reading material down, leaving it open to one of my favourite passages. I had to focus on the job at hand: controlling traffic flow on Interstate 95.

Flipping on my Virginia state police car's flashing lights, I accelerated. The offenders quickly pulled over. I slowed and cruised in behind them. My lights shone through their rear window, illuminating an elderly couple. I got out and began walking towards the other car. Unlike some motorists, with two senior citizens I wasn't too concerned about the possibility of them assaulting me or pulling a gun. However, another threat stalked me in the pitch-black night air. I never saw it coming.

From behind me a Chrysler car came off the motorway and collided with the stationary car. The bonnet emblem from the Chrysler was embedded in my back. I was caught between the stationary car and the Chrysler.

From here on, not everything I will tell you about this incident is based on personal recollection. Parts have been reconstructed from paramedics, rescue squad members, doctors, troopers and medical examiner's data. The evidence is documented.

After being slapped like a pinball between the vehicles, I flew up into the air. Coming back down, I landed on the roof of the Chrysler. The top half of my body fell onto the motorway. Just then, two fully loaded, 80,000-pound tractor trailers steamed up the northbound lane, travelling close together. The first driver saw me in time to jerk his rig out of the way without jack-knifing or running me over. The second trailer had little time to react. And he couldn't turn 80,000 pounds at a 45-degree angle that fast. Throwing his hands up in front on his face, he cried, 'Oh, my God!'

'Trooper, you'll never believe what happened!' he blurted out later to the investigating officer. 'You'll never believe it! All of a sudden the wheel on my tractor turned to the left and back to the right. Trooper, I never touched that wheel!' Humanly speaking, what happened was impossible. However, the people whom I stopped for speeding weren't as excited.

Regaining consciousness, I got up and I wandered about 25 steps up the shoulder and collapsed. Soon after, the rescue squad arrived. In vain they tried to get a heartbeat or a faint pulse. After 30 minutes of trying to find vital signs, at 10.23 p.m. they covered my face with a sheet. Then they turned their attentions to cleaning up from the accident. With my body headed for the local morgue, they weren't in a big rush.

Thank God I had been prepared for this moment long before. Because of my father's influence, I had believed in Jesus since childhood. Despite a fourth-grade education, Dad had more wisdom than a roomful of PhDs who don't know the Lord. He didn't have a college degree, but he built his own house and car from the ground up. He also designed furniture.

Raised on a farm, near my present home, I was sometimes ridiculed as a dumb country boy. 'I know why you believe the way you do, Buddy,' a man once told me. 'If you had just a little bit of education, you wouldn't believe like you do.' Thanks to my track skills (I missed going to the Olympic trials by three-tenths of a second), an athletic scholarship paid for that education. But I'll never forget what Dad told me the day I left for college.

'Son, go ahead and get your education,' he said quietly. 'But education will not give you the joy and peace you're looking for. Only God can do that.'

'What do you mean, Dad?'

'You take a truck loaded full of watermelons and a thief, and a thief will steal the watermelons off the truck. You educate him and he'll steal the watermelons *and* the truck. But he's still a thief. Education didn't change him.'

I thank the Lord for a man like my father. He has supported me in my job. Police work is stressful and different shifts and job tension take their toll on many cops and their families. My grandmother influenced me too. She had a huge smile which seemed to swallow her face. I remember coming up on our porch as a boy. She'd be sitting here swinging, reading her Bible, tears streaming down her face.

'Grandma, are you okay?' I'd ask.

'I sure am,' she always smiled.

I was with my 72-year-old grandma the night she died. So weak and sick she couldn't lift her arms, she could barely move a hand. The night she stepped into Glory, she looked up and said, 'All those lights. All those people.'

'Grandma, the lights are off,' I said softly. 'There's no one here but you and me.'

Then with her last ounce of energy, she lifted her right hand up, smiled and said, 'I know who that is.' It took me years to understand what she meant. What helped me grasp it was the experience I had before coming back to life. The encounter will remain with me forever.

Everything went pitch black after I passed out on the highway that night. It was the darkest black I had ever seen. I felt like I was trapped in a deep hole. Yet I felt no fear or pain. Emerging from this charcoal air were thousands upon thousands of hands from the wrist down. They came at me in waves, grabbing at my body but never touching me.

I've been asked what this was before I ever discussed this publicly. In giving my testimony, I asked God to help me not to mislead anyone in explaining it. For what I endured, I believe, was the valley of the shadow of death. As the 23rd Psalm says: 'Yea, though I walk through the valley of the shadow of death, I will fear no evil, for thou art with me.' One day you too will walk through that valley. If you are a Christian, Satan can grab all he wants. I believe that's what he was trying to do that night, along with his angels. Vainly trying to make one last snatch at God's child. Those hands fluttered at me for what seemed like two or three minutes. Then I found myself bathed in a very bright light. The whitest, brightest light I had ever seen. When I looked around, it was just as white above me as it was in the distance.

Have you ever had one of those times when you felt like you could reach up and touch a piece of Heaven? Ever felt like you were going to burst wide open? Just didn't know what you would do? Multiply that a thousandfold and you may have some idea of the unspeakable joy I felt as I stood there. Glory, happiness and peace filled my soul. I know now why we will need a new body when we get to Heaven. Our Earthly ones won't be able to contain the radiance.

Ahead in the distance I saw a large door. It looked like a thousand rainbows were pouring out of that door. It was the most beautiful sight I've ever seen, the most dazzling colours (and with four children and 50 boxes of crayons around the house, I know my colours). Attracted by the sight, I began walking towards it.

As I drew closer, I felt like the joy would cause my body to split in two. I felt inadequate trying to paint you a picture of this scene. God says in His Word (1 Corinthians 2:9) that we haven't seen or heard the things He has prepared for us. It's true!

Had I made it to that door, I believe my loved ones would have read my obituary and mourned my passing. Meanwhile, I would be dancing on the hills of Glory, wrapping my arms around Moses and Abraham, and rejoicing in His presence. However, when I got within six feet of the door I woke up. It's been more than 12 years since this happened, and for a long time I was petrified to tell anyone about it.

For some reason, God brought me back to life 23 minutes after I was pronounced dead at the scene of the crash. When I woke up, they were wheeling my body down the hallway toward the morgue's cold storage area. A trooper named Sonny Dobbins (who has since died) was clutching the railing of the cart. Sonny was a mountain of a man. I had never seen him cry before. He was now.

As I was trying to yank the sheet off my face, I saw the lights in the hallway. Blood had matted it to my face, so it was hard to remove. When I finally got the sheet off, I had no idea what had transpired. Looking at my fellow trooper, I asked, 'Sonny, what happened?'

After his mouth fell open, he stammered, 'Ah, ah, ah, ah ... Bud, you're supposed to be dead!'

Suddenly everyone jumped into action. Instead of cold storage, they whisked me to the hospital. I was hospitalized and later spent three months recuperating at home. I also had $1,200 worth of plastic surgery done on my face. It didn't really change much – I still have a big nose and baggy eyes. But they closed my facial wounds so there wouldn't be scars.

Remember I said that I was 'out' for 23 minutes? After four minutes without oxygen you're supposed to have brain damage.

The 'bottom line' – I'm still healthy, running and working out. Still working in law enforcement, stopping speeders, arresting lawbreakers ... and defending myself when I must. That doesn't always call for a gun.

One night death stared me directly in the eye again. A criminal stood with a pistol pointed at my head. Without even thinking I said, 'To be absent from the body is to be present with the Lord' (2 Corinthians 5:8). Putting the gun down, the old boy looked at me and said, 'You're crazy. You can't be "the man"' (a slang expression for police). After we shook hands I arrested him.

Remember the book I was reading on the Thanksgiving Eve I nearly died? It was the Bible. The page was turned to Romans 8:28: 'We know that in everything God works for good with those who love Him, who are called according to His purpose' (RSV).

If you don't know the joy of Someone working on your behalf, invite Jesus to live in your heart today. He can take away all fear, no matter what frightens you. And He can remove all your pain, no matter how intense. Even when a car slams into you on a motorway.

5 RICHARD

Friends are an important part of most people's lives. When Richard, a schoolboy living in Ghana, became ill, he could have had no idea how vital friendship with Christians of his own age would prove to be. But they had faith to pray for him when they came to visit him in hospital one day and found the curtains drawn around his bed.

There was a boy named Richard who was at school in Ho in the 1970s. He had become a born-again Christian through the activities of the Scripture Union in his school. His father, who was a fetish priest, did not take kindly to his conversion. When he discovered that Richard had become a Christian he refused to pay for any more school because Richard, as a Christian, would not want to serve in the shrine of his father. So it seemed that the boy would have to stop his secondary education. But by grace of the Lord, some friends agreed to help pay his fees and so he continued up to the fifth form.

Some time after this happened he was taken ill. He reported to the local hospital and was admitted. Christian friends used to visit him in the ward. One afternoon when his friends came to visit, the nurse on duty would not allow them to see him. They noticed that Richard's bed was surrounded by a green screen. The green screen is suggestive of one of two things – a bed bath or death. His Christian friends persisted with their request, but the nurse would allow only two of them to see him. When they were behind the screen, they saw to their dismay that Richard had died. Without any hesitation, they started praying for him. In their prayer, they asked the Lord if it was His will that Richard should pass away at this time.

A few minutes later, they noticed Richard's arm move. Then his other hand also moved. The friends were watching keenly. Thirdly, his eyes opened and he sighed very deeply. 'Ah! I am sorry to be back in this world again,' he said. The friends asked him what he meant by that, and this is the story he told them.

'I was thrown into the air like a bullet from a gun. I was moving into the sky until a hole opened in the sky for me to enter. When I entered, I saw a small boy in a white dress who held my hand and said "Welcome." He took me in and asked me to look back at the Earth and to see what was happening upon it. When I looked down, behold, the Earth was like a ball, with people upon it. Men and women were committing shameless things which can hardly be imagined. The boy remarked that the life men live on Earth is visible from that place.

'The boy told me to follow him, which I did. We reached a place where a long line of people appeared in front of a Judge sitting on a throne. There were some people there whom I recognized. People were taking turns to come into the presence of the Judge (2 Corinthians 5:10). Watching them, I saw that some people came before the Judge and began to plead that they did not know that one day they would appear before Him for judgement. The Judge looked down while each person made their plea. After pleading each took a cap and found themselves moving to the left of the Judge. Some people came into the Judge's presence and never said a word, but stepped out and passed the right-hand side of the Judge.'

Richard continued: 'I had been watching this scene for some time when the angelic boy asked me to accompany him to see what was happening to those who passed on the left side of the Judge. When we went there was a door standing before us. The boy knocked at the door and it opened. The room was very dark and those inside were weeping and groaning and gnashing their teeth. I got so scared that I began to pity them. The boy took me back to see those who were passing on the right. We again came to a door. The boy knocked at the door and it opened. Looking inside, I saw the floor was all gold. The whole place was very bright and the people were rejoicing and singing praises to the Lord of Lords. It was full of joy. I got so excited that I jumped to enter in, but the boy held me back. He told me my turn had not yet come.

'The boy then brought me back to where to took me in. He asked whether I had ever read Matthew 24. I said I had. He added that the signs for the Second Coming of the Lord are being fulfilled one after another. He said it would not be long before He would appear and then told me to testify of what I had seen to whoever I could. The angelic boy then left me and I am here on Earth again.'

6 KENNETH HAGIN

Kenneth Hagin thought that by the time he was nine he had done all that was necessary to get a place in Heaven. But it was only later that he found out the truth.

I was born and raised Southern Baptist. I thought the Lord Jesus Christ and all of His disciples were Southern Baptist. It came as a real shock to me when I found out that they weren't.

I read the Bible one day and decided that Paul couldn't have been Baptist, because he said 'I thank my God I speak with tongues...' (1 Corinthians 14:18). I had never heard any Baptist say that!

Being born and raised Southern Baptist, I felt sorry for everybody who wasn't Baptist. But you know, friends, you can be a church member and not be a Christian.

Even though I'm a member of a church and believe in going to church, just going to church won't save you or make you a Christian, any more than going to the barn will make you a cow! Being a member of a church won't make you a Christian any more than being a member of a country club will make you a Christian. You have to be born again.

We've got too many people who think they're a Christian just because they're a member of a church.

I joined the church when I was nine years old. The reason I joined was because my Sunday School teacher said to all of us boys one Sunday morning, 'How many of you want to go to Heaven?' Well, every one of us wanted to go to Heaven. So the Sunday school teacher said, 'When the pastor, Dr So-and-so, gives the invitation this morning, you just go down to the front.'

Since we all wanted to go to Heaven, when the invitation was given, several of us marched right down to the front and shook hands with the preacher. We joined the church and were baptized in water. And I really, actually, thought I was a Christian.

Later, when I got into an evangelistic-type service – even one sponsored by my own church – and the Spirit of God began to deal with me about being saved, I'd say to myself, *I'm already saved. I belong to the church. I've been baptized in water. I'm already a Christian.*

I was born prematurely with a deformed heart. I weighed less than two pounds at birth. In my day, more than 75 years ago, they didn't have incubators to put premature babies in, so my possibility of living was practically nil. Nevertheless, I did survive, but I never ran and played like other little children. I never had a normal childhood.

When I was 15 years old, I became totally bedridden. Five doctors said I had to die: I couldn't live. But it was there, on my sick bed, that I was born again on the 22nd day of April, 1933 in the south bedroom of 405 North College Street in the city of McKinney, Texas. It was 20 minutes to 8 o'clock on a Saturday night.

This south bedroom had a fireplace. Grandpa had a clock on the mantelpiece. My mother, grandmother and youngest brother, Pat, were sitting there in the room with me, for I had taken a turn for the worse. The doctor had been called (remember, in 1933, doctors made house calls).

Just as Grandpa's clock struck 7.30, my heart stopped beating within my bosom.

And I could feel, faster than you could snap your fingers, the blood cease to circulate way down at the end of my toes. My toes seemed to go numb. This numbness spread to my feet, my ankles, my knees, my hips, my stomach, my heart – and I *leaped* out of my body.

I did not lose consciousness: I leaped out of my body like a diver would leap off a diving board into a swimming pool. I knew I was outside my body. I could see my family in the room, but I couldn't contact them.

I had it in my mind to say goodbye to Momma, Granny and my little brother, but I leaped out of my body before I could get the words out fully.

I began to descend – down, down, into a pit, like you'd go down into a well, cavern or cave. I did not know that my physical voice picked that up. As I was trying to say goodbye, I knew I was going down into that place. All three of my family members who were present testified later, 'When you said goodbye, your voice sounded like you were way down in a cave or cavern or something.'

And I continued to descend. I went down feet first – down, down, down, down. I could look up and see the lights of the Earth. They finally faded away. Darkness encompassed me round about – darkness that is blacker than any night man has ever seen. It seemed that if you had a knife, you could cut a chunk of it out. You couldn't see your hand if it was one inch in front of your nose.

The farther down I went, the darker it became – and the hotter it became – until finally, way down beneath me, I could see fingers of light playing on the wall of darkness. And I came to the bottom of the pit.

This happened to me more than 60 years ago, yet it's just as real to me as if it had happened the week before last. Spiritual things never grow old.

When I came to the bottom of the pit, I saw what caused the fingers of light to play on the wall of darkness. Out in front of me, beyond the gates or the entrance into Hell, I saw giant, great orange flames with a white crest.

I was pulled toward Hell just like a magnet pulls metal unto itself. I knew that once I entered through those gates, I could not come back. I endeavoured to slow down my descent, because when I came to the bottom of the pit, there still was a slant downward.

I was conscious of the fact that some kind of creature met me at the bottom of that pit. I didn't look at it. My gaze was riveted on the gates, yet I knew that a creature was there by my right side.

I didn't know until a good many years later, when I discovered it in the Book of Isaiah, that the Bible says, 'Hell from beneath is moved for thee at thy coming: it stirreth up the dead for thee...' (Isaiah 14:9).

That creature, when I endeavoured to slow down my descent, took me by the arm to escort me in. When he did, away above the blackness and the darkness a voice spoke. It sounded like a male voice, but I don't know what he said. I don't know whether it was God, Jesus, an angel or who. He did not speak in the English language: it was a foreign language.

That place just shook at the few words he spoke! And the creature took his hand off my arm. There was a power like a suction to my back parts that pulled me back. I floated away from the entrance to Hell until I stood in the shadows. Then, like a suction from above, I floated up, head first, through the darkness.

Before I got to the top, I could see the light. I've been down in a well: it was like you were way down in a well and could see the light up above.

I came up on the porch of my grandpa's house. We lived in one of those old-fashioned houses they used to build down in Texas, with a porch nearly all the way around the house. I came up on the south side of the house. I could see Grandpa's porch swing there. I could see the giant cedar trees in the yard. I stood there on the porch just for a second.

Then I went through the wall – not through the door, and not through the window – through the wall, and seemed to leap inside my body like a man would slip his foot inside his boot in the morning time.

Before I leaped inside my body, I could see my grandmother sitting on the edge of the bed holding me in her arms. When I got inside my body, I could communicate with her.

I said to her – and I don't know how I knew it – 'Granny, I'm going again, and I won't be back.'

She said, 'Son, I thought you weren't coming back that time!'

I looked around the room and my mother was not there.

She said, 'Son, I told your mother you were gone, and she rushed out of the door, praying.'

And then I heard her. She was over on the north side of the house. She came back around the porch, praying at the top of her voice.

People told me later that they could hear her crying and praying for blocks around.

When I said, 'I want to tell Momma goodbye,' my grandmother called to her, 'Lillie!' but she couldn't make her hear, because Momma was praying so loud.

If you're not ready to go, you want somebody with you. You're afraid! I said, 'Granny, don't leave me! Don't leave me! I'm afraid I'll go while you're gone! I want somebody with me! Don't leave me!' And so she gathered me in her arms again.

And I said, 'Tell Momma I said goodbye. Tell Momma I love her. Tell Momma I appreciate her staying with us.' (My daddy left us when I was six years of age, and Momma was left with four children to look after. With all the trouble she had had, and being just a baby Christian and not knowing how to cast her burden upon the Lord, she had had a complete mental and physical breakdown.)

I felt myself slipping. I said, 'Granny, I'm going again. You've been a second mother to me when Momma was ill.'

We four children went to live with different relatives when our mother became ill. I went to live with my grandmother on my mother's side of the family. My grandmother used to always call me 'my boy', and she'd always say, 'Kiss me right there – kiss me right there.'

So I kissed her on the cheek and said goodbye.

My heart stopped for the second time. It's almost as real to me today, over half a century later, as it was that day.

I could feel the blood cease to circulate. The tips of my toes went numb – then my feet, ankles, knees, hips, stomach and heart. I leaped out of my body and began to descend: down, down, down. Oh, I know it was just a few seconds, but it seemed like an eternity.

Down, until the darkness encompassed me round about. The lights above faded away. The farther down I went, the hotter and darker it became, until I came again to the bottom of the pit and saw the entrance to Hell, or the gates as I call it. I was conscious that that creature met me.

I endeavoured to slow down my descent – it seemed like I was floating down – yet it seemed like there was a pull that pulled me downward. And that creature took me by the arm. When he did, that voice spoke again – a man's voice. It was a foreign language. I don't know what he said, but when he spoke, that whole place just shook. That creature took his hand off my arm.

It was like suction to my back. I never turned around. I just came floating back into the shadows of darkness. And then I was pulled up, head first. I could see the lights of the Earth above me before I came up out of the pit. The only difference this time was that I came up at the foot of the bed.

The first time I had come up on the porch. This time I came up at the foot of the bed. For a second time I stood there. I could see my body lying there on the bed. I could see Grandma as she sat there holding me in her arms. I seemed to leap from the foot of the bed inside my body through my mouth. When I got back inside my body, I could communicate with Granny. I said, 'Granny, I'm going again, and I won't be back this time.'

She said again, 'Son, I thought you weren't coming back that time.'

I said, 'Granny, where is Grandpa? I want to tell Grandpa goodbye.'

She said, 'Son, you know your grandad went down to the east part of town to collect rent off some of his rent houses.'

'Oh,' I said, 'I remember that now.'

I said, 'Granny, tell Grandpa goodbye. I've never known what it means to have a daddy. He's been the nearest to a daddy I've known. He gave me a home when I had none. Tell him I love him. Tell Grandpa that I said goodbye.'

Then I left a word for my only sister, the oldest child, and my oldest brother, and then I said, 'Where's Pat?' Pat was my little brother, nine years old.

Granny said, 'Well, he ran next door and called the doctor again.'

I left a word for each one of them, and my heart stopped for the third time.

I could feel the circulation as it cut off. Suddenly my toes went numb. Faster than you can snap your fingers, my toes, feet, ankles, knees, hips, stomach and heart went dead – and I leaped out of my body and began to descend.

Until this time, I thought, *this is not happening to me. This is just a hallucination. It can't be real!*

But then I thought, *This is the third time. I won't come back this time! I won't come back this time!* Darkness encompassed me round about, darker than any night man has ever seen. The Bible talks about men and women being cast into 'outer darkness' where there is 'weeping and gnashing of teeth' (Matthew 8:12).

And in the darkness, I cried out, 'God! I belong to the church! I've been baptized in water!' (You see, I was telling Him, 'I shouldn't be going this direction: I'm going the wrong direction!')

I waited for an answer, but there was no answer; only the echo of my own voice through the darkness. And the second time I cried a little louder, 'God! I belong to the church! I've been baptized in water!'

I waited for an answer, but there was no answer; only the echo of my own voice as it echoed through the darkness.

I would scare a congregation out of their wits if I ever imitated the way I screamed the third time, although if I could scare them out of Hell and into Heaven, I'd do it. I'd flat do it!

I literally screamed, 'God! God! I belong to the church! I've been baptized in water!' But you see, although being baptized in water is right, although belonging to the church is right, it takes more than belonging to the church and more than being baptized in water to miss Hell and go to Heaven!

And all I heard was the echo of my own voice as it echoed through the darkness.

I came again to the bottom of that pit. Again I could feel the heat as it beat me in the face. Again I approached the entrance, the gates into Hell itself. That creature took me by the arm. I intended to put up a fight, if I could, to keep from going in. I only managed to slow down my descent just a little, and he took me by the arm.

Thank God that voice spoke. I don't know who it was – I didn't see anybody – I just heard the voice. I don't know what he said, but whatever he said, that place shook; it just trembled. And that creature took his hand off my arm.

It was just like there was suction to my back parts. It pulled me back, away from the entrance to Hell, until I stood in the shadows. Then it pulled me up head first.

As I was going up through the darkness, I began to pray. My spirit, the man who lives inside this physical body, is an eternal being; a spirit man. I began to pray: 'O God! I come to You in the Name of the Lord Jesus Christ. I ask You to forgive me of my sins and to cleanse me from all sin.'

I came up beside the bed. The difference between the three experiences was that I came up on the porch the first time; I came up at the foot of the bed the second time; and I came up right beside the bed the third time and leaped right inside my body.

When I got inside my body, my physical voice picked up my prayer right in the middle of the sentence. I was already praying out of my spirit; my physical voice picked up my prayer and continued to pray.

I want you to know that it was just like a two-ton weight lifted off my chest. Peace came on the inside. I looked at Grandpa's old clock on the mantelpiece, and it said 20 minutes till 8 o'clock. All of that happened in 10 minutes.

So I was born again at 20 minutes till 8 o'clock on 22 April, 1933 in the south bedroom, and I've been saved ever since.

I was still bedridden, and the doctor said that I had to die. In fact, five doctors said that I had to die.

But I'll tell you what I did. I praised myself to sleep every night. All the lights would be out in the house; everybody would be in bed. I'd be left alone, just a boy of 15, with my own thoughts.

I said, 'They may find me dead in bed in the morning, but, oh, I'm so glad that I didn't go to Hell!'

At night, I'd start saying quietly to myself: 'Thank you, Jesus. Glory to God. Praise the Lord. I'm going to put a smile on my face.'

Rev. Kenneth Hagin Ministries may be contacted at the following address:

Kenneth Hagin Ministries
PO Box 50126
Tulsa
OK 74150-0126
USA

7 LORRAINE TUTMARC

Lorraine Tutmarc was very ill with peritonitis. During her Near Death Experience she was rescued by Jesus from the River of Death, and visited Heaven.

When I was 22 years old, in the spring of 1928, I was pregnant with my third child. Unfortunately I had a miscarriage and efforts to remove the tissue were unsuccessful. Peritonitis set in, causing blood poisoning. My condition rapidly deteriorated. Although I went to the hospital several times, they sent me home on each occasion saying there was nothing they could do. Antibiotics were not yet available. I can remember my doctor visiting our house at regular intervals, asking my husband in a voice that was unfortunately too loud, 'Has she gone yet?' For about three months I had pain throughout my body, was almost too weak to move, couldn't eat, and required intra-venous feeding.

One morning I awoke and noticed almost a numb feeling from my head down. All the pain was gone. And then, slowly, I was rising from the bed. I felt an immediate, terrific sense of freedom, as though I'd just taken off a heavy coat. I was float-ing and euphoric with peace. But I can also remember asking myself, 'How did I do this?' I looked down on my body, which appeared to be sleeping. Nearby I saw the doctor, the nurse and my husband, who was sitting next to my bed. Then, from the upper corner of the room, I began to move backwards. I glanced at my physical body. It was the last thing I saw as I went through the wall.

I found myself in a region of total darkness up to my neck in water. My bodily pain, absent moments before, had returned. The water was very cold and moving around. I was quite panicky because I cannot swim. In my mind I asked, 'Where am I?' In response I heard a loud, loving and beautiful voice, sounding almost as though it came from a megaphone, saying, 'This is eternity! This is eternity! You are lost! You are lost!' In some way I knew that was God's voice. 'What is this?' I again asked in my mind. God's reply was, 'This is the river of death.'

Struggling in the darkness I suddenly found myself being carried into the upper portions of a large whirlpool. I fought to keep my head above water, but gradually was drawn lower into the pool where the water was whirling more quickly. By the time I was sucked into the bottom of the pool I was completely exhausted. Emotionally, fear and hopelessness had drained me. So, as I was going underwater for what I was sure was the last time, I completely gave up! It was then that I saw light enter the water around me. The water turned warm.

I turned, looked up and there was Jesus, about four feet above me. I was staring at the most beautiful person I've ever seen. The love I sensed coming from Him was beyond description. Light coming from Him lit up the entire area around me, but He was so wonderful to look at that I kept watching Him. His robe was pale ivory, with a red blotch in the chest area. His hair was auburn coloured, shoulder length. But it was a look in those eyes that I could not turn away from, which I will not forget. They were large, full of meaning and kind. While loving, the gaze was also penetrating, a look that said that He knew everything I'd ever done, and everything I could ever do, both bad and good, and that no matter what, He would always be there. I could count on Him. His love would never fail.

I remember wondering about the red blotch on the robe, and the same deep loving voice I had heard earlier said that it represented the blood Jesus had shed for us on the cross. In the background I heard what sounded like millions of tiny bells whose sound had the purest tone. Throughout the rest of my near-death experience they were always detectable as a distant presence.

Then in a voice that was powerful and loving He said, 'Follow Me.' I answered, 'Yes, I will.' Instantly the water disappeared. He lowered His right hand and held my left. His hand was warm; then I felt the power of God moving through my body. And I'd never heard of the power of God! It was like sparks from smitten steel you could say, just coming right through my body, from my head to my toes, over and over again. As it came I grew stronger and stronger, until finally I thought, 'I'm well! I have no more pain! This is real!'

I rose so that I was next to Jesus. Although I was still holding His hand, He had turned and I followed His gaze. Both of us seemed to float toward a gold wall that stretched as far as the eye could see in either direction. Around us I felt a warm breeze carrying with it a scent of flowers. We stopped perhaps fifteen feet away. I noticed that the golden wall, which was about nine feet high, was transparent to a depth of about eight inches.

Around me it seemed like the dawn of a new day, as though it was about 5 a.m. From behind the wall I sensed activity. Things were happening. This was something felt rather than heard and I noticed it until the end of my NDE. I began to hear birds singing and chirping. As I listened to them for several minutes, their number and volume increased, then died away. String instruments then began to play enchantingly. Their volume and number also grew slowly, then disappeared. Finally,

I heard a heavenly choir of the most beautiful harmonized voices singing in a minor key. They too grew in number, until hundreds of voices were apparent. I was captivated and drawn toward this realm. It seemed that the music spoke to me and welcomed me. I was still holding Jesus' hand, but stepped toward the wall to search for a gate or door. None was apparent. I turned back to look at Jesus. He was gone.

I felt myself return into my body, going back the same way I had come. When I opened my eyes the doctor, nurse and my husband were around me. I exclaimed, 'I've seen the Lord! I've been to Heaven!' I repeated this and added, 'I'm healed! I'm healed!' I can remember my husband staring at me and trying to restrain me. I was extremely hungry and insisted on eating something. Despite protests from the doctor, I eventually enjoyed my first meal of tea, toast and asparagus. I can remember the doctor saying, 'I've always been an atheist, but now I've seen a miracle.' Two weeks later I was painting the inside of my house. I never had a pain after that.

This experience was not one that I was searching for nor expecting; I hadn't been to church since I was quite young, nor had I ever read the Bible. For me it was an intensely personal experience that went far beyond the boundaries of denominational religion. It also led to my awareness of God's presence in the world and an insatiable hunger to read the Bible.

Occasionally, I find myself waking in the middle of the night and hear for a short period of time the sound of those bells I first heard during my near-death experience.

Editor's note: Lorraine left this world several years ago, but while she was alive here she brought hope, love and inspiration into the lives of many.

This story is published with the kind permission of Seattle IANDS, PO Box 84333, Seattle, WA 98124, USA, and may be found on the Internet at the following web site address: www.seattleiands.org.

8 DR TERRY ELDER

Doctors have to be ready for anything – but the emergency case that Dr Terry Elder dealt with one night in Texas had an unusual and heart-warming ending.

'Dr Elder to the trauma centre!' The announcement came suddenly over the intercom on what, up to that time, had been a relatively quiet evening at my local hospital. There were no ambulances out on call that we were aware of, and I had just stepped down the hall to the doctors' lounge for a snack. A sudden call like that usually meant one thing – someone had arrived by private vehicle, in acute distress, rather than by the usual ambulance transport.

This could often be a myocardial infarction (heart attack), severe respiratory distress or a sick infant. Occasionally it would be a knife or gun injury that occurred near the hospital, but you could always be sure of one thing with a call like this – it would be a true emergency.

As I entered the trauma suite seconds later, there was a female patient in her late twenties with two stab wounds in her left anterior chest, directly over her heart! She was in an extremely unstable condition and was breathing sporadically. As I established the airway by intubating her, the nurses were completing their initial phase of treatment that included intravenous lines, monitors, lab work and initial vital signs. I thought how fortunate it was to have such a good and experienced trauma team in a state-of-the-art trauma treatment facility. During the next few moments it became obvious that the patient was not stabilizing, but was deteriorating. Even more ominous, she was developing symptoms that could only mean one thing – cardiac tamponade.

This is a condition where a penetrating wound to the heart produces bleeding into the sac that surrounds the heart, thereby compressing the heart and inhibiting its life-sustaining pumping action. The patient's blood pressure was steadily dropping, and I turned to the head nurse and asked for the thoracotomy tray and instruments.

In the speciality of emergency medicine, the 'open thoracotomy' is probably the most dramatic procedure and involves making an incision between the fifth and sixth ribs in order to expose the heart, lungs and major vessels in an effort to control bleeding. This is the procedure we initiated, and as I lifted the lung to expose the heart, it was obvious that this was indeed cardiac tamponade. By making an incision in the membranes of the sac surrounding the heart, the pressure was relieved and the heart was able to function. By this time, the heart had been unable to beat for about two minutes due to compression, and an intracardiac injection of adrenaline was needed to 'jump start' the heart.

This was accomplished and the patient's vital signs returned with a pulse of about 100 and a blood pressure of 120/80. However, the stab wound continued to bleed, so this necessitated continual release of rebuilding pressure by keeping my fingers over the incision and allowing a release every several minutes. This went on for about 20 minutes while we awaited the arrival of the thoracic surgeon and the operating room was being prepared. When everything was ready, we moved the patient to the operating room, all the while with my hand in her chest to allow continual release of reoccurring pressure of the pericardial sac.

The surgery went smoothly. The stab wound to the heart was repaired and the patient was sent to the intensive care unit. I returned to my duties in the trauma centre. Later that evening my curiosity got the better of me and I asked her if she remembered anything from her clinical death experience of several minutes. She was still intubated and on a ventilator and thus could not speak, but she shook her head no. The look in her eyes and squeeze of my hand told me she was very grateful to be alive.

Several weeks later I received a very nice thank you letter from the patient and her mother. Her mother made the comment that she knew that the Lord was guiding me that night, and I wholeheartedly agreed, as things had gone very smoothly and her recovery had been remarkable. The thank you was deeply appreciated, but I was not prepared for the rest of the story.

About six weeks later, late one evening, a woman in her late twenties arrived in the trauma centre with her young daughter and requested to see me. At first I did not recognize her, as I had not seen her since visiting her in the Intensive Care Unit, but it was that former patient who was now completely recovered. As we began to talk, she related the most amazing story to me and the nursing staff, many of whom did not know the Lord.

She said, 'After you left that evening when you visited me in the Intensive Care Unit I drifted back to sleep and awakened the next morning as the hospital chaplain was giving the morning devotion over the intercom.

'As he concluded his prayer, instantly, it was as though a light came on and I remembered what had happened. I remembered the stabbing and being driven the six blocks to the hospital while in excruciating pain. As we pulled into the ambulance ramp, it was as though I fell asleep and began to slide down a long tunnel with a bright light at the end. When I got to the end, I was at a crossroads. I looked down and I could see footprints, much like the painting of *Footprints In The Sand*. As I followed the path of the footprints to where they ended, I looked up and there stood Jesus! The love and compassion of His countenance was indescribable, and He told me that it was not yet my time and that I was to go back to Earth. The next thing I remember was waking up in the Intensive Care Unit.'

As she concluded, I asked her when she had accepted the Lord as her Saviour. I was surprised once again, as she related that as a young girl she had been active in Sunday school. However, as she grew up she fell away from the Lord, and was very far away and back-slidden at the time of this stabbing. Since this near-death incident, her uncle, who was a strong Christian, had been witnessing to her and praying for her, and she stated she was now very close to committing her life to the Lord. As she concluded, the Holy Spirit did not lead me to do anything in regards to praying with her, but He did give me a word. I related it to her. 'You will soon become a Christian and know the Lord personally.' She thanked us all again, and with her little daughter in hand, left the trauma centre.

I was thrilled when I contacted her recently. Now, nearly two years after the incident, she has been born again (see John 3:3), made Jesus the Lord of her life, and is actively involved in church life. Six months ago she was water-baptized. She was again so thankful for what the Lord had done and commented that at the time of her near-death experience she would have gone to Hell if she had died.

The purpose of this testimony is certainly not to give any credit or glory to this doctor, but to give the glory to whom glory is due, and that is to the true hero of this story, Jesus Christ. The Word says, 'But from everlasting to everlasting the

Lord's love is with those who fear Him, and His righteousness with their children's children' (Psalms 103:17 NIV), and this is the overriding truth in this case. I have often thought of the fact that she was having this experience 'on the other side', totally unknown to me, at the time that I had my hand on her heart during the thoracotomy and resuscitation.

How many times have we been unaware of the Lord's intervention in our own lives – the 'close calls' that may have been 'crossroad' experiences? How many times has God in His mercy reached out and supernaturally brought us back into the mainstream centre of His will?

In my own experience of salvation as a freshman in college, there was not a single day I could look back on as the time and place where I received Christ as my personal Saviour. There is, however, a period of time where I came to know Him and where I turned my life over to Him to use as He would. I was later baptized in His Holy Spirit and through college, marriage, medical school and now the mission field, I can truly say that 'the Lord's love is from everlasting to everlasting'.

As a final note, I have always had a lifelong love of flying. Prior to college I had applied to the air force and navy, but was turned down due to an astigmatism in my right eye. Halfway through medical school I found out about a medical waiver and I was taking flying lessons a month later. Now, with several thousand hours ATP (Airline Transport Rating), commercial, instrument, multi, etc, the Lord has allowed me to combine medicine and flying in our ministry, Grace Aire Medical Foundation.

We are dedicated to providing humanitarian and Christian relief to Third World situations and we have seen many come to Christ. Truly I can say the Lord has given me the desires of my heart as He prepared me for ministry.

9 MARIA POLACK

Maria Polack hadn't been feeling too well the night she got up to use the bathroom – but she could not have known that, due to a fall which rendered her unconscious, she would in fact leave this world and have an encounter with Jesus.

I was born in Portugal, during the time that it was under the rule of a dictator. My parents were Catholic, but because the dictatorship and the Catholic Church were linked in many people's eyes, I had little interest in the Catholic Church, although from a very young age I loved God. I wanted to know about the Holy Spirit, but nobody in my parish church seemed to be able to tell me anything, so I went around searching. It was years later, however, before God broke through into my life, in a way I could not have believed in a thousand years.

It was a typical warm Portuguese night, but I had woken up in discomfort and I knew that I was going to have to get up to go to the bathroom. I had reached the age of 26, and I had been feeling unwell for some time, and had started to pass blood. Sometimes I would feel faint, and on some occasions I actually did faint. The problem was, I knew that if I got up, I would probably wake my parents. I was staying with them at the time, and being that much older than I, I knew that they needed their sleep. In the end, though, there was nothing I could do. Like it or not, I had to get up, and I made my way to the bathroom as silently as I could, closing all the doors behind me, so as to make as little noise as possible.

I'm still not too clear about just exactly what happened next, but I must have stumbled as I entered the bathroom, or perhaps I fainted again. But the result was that I hit my head hard on a marble corner in the bathroom. I had fainted and become unconscious before – and since. But this time was very different from those other times. Suddenly I found myself going through a large tunnel, at great speed. What could be happening? I was travelling so fast that I could hear a loud whooshing sound as I moved along.

As I travelled, I realized that I was moving towards a source of light. This light was more beautiful than anything I had ever seen on Earth. It was a wonderful golden colour – more beautiful than anything I had ever experienced even on the sunniest day in Portugal.

Then I went through an entrance where the light was. The atmosphere was totally serene, and I was now surrounded completely by the wonderful golden light. At this point I had no idea what was happening to me, but I felt safe, secure and very peaceful. I felt a presence near to me, and realized that it was coming from the middle of this wonderful light. The light was very intense, although it did not hurt my eyes. I was aware of so much love surrounding me, a love the type of which I have never experienced before. I knew that this love was far greater than anything that any human could generate, however much they tried. I began to realise that the presence within this light knew everything there was to know about me, and yet loved me totally. I could not see who it was that was in the centre of this light, although I guessed by now that it must be either Jesus or God Himself. This was strange, because as I have explained, I had been brought up in the Catholic faith but God had played little or no part in my life, although I had always wanted to know more about Him.

Then my whole life started to be shown to me. I saw the good parts and the bad parts. I didn't feel condemned, even when I saw myself do or think things that I should not have done or thought. I knew that He understood what had made me do those things at the time. I knew that He loved me, in spite of everything that I had ever done. We started to have a conversation together, although no words were spoken. It was just a conversation within the mind. I could hear His words in my head, and I found it easy to communicate in this way. When I saw myself doing the things that I should not have done, I felt very sad and repentant, especially as I was experiencing so much of His love at the time. I felt consoled, and I did not ever want to leave the place where I was, even though I had a young child who obviously needed my care and attention at that time.

I was aware of other things around me – I think I was standing near to a tree, but I was concentrating too much on the Lord and what He was saying and showing me to bother too much about what was around me. Then He said that I must go back – it wasn't time for me to be with Him permanently yet. I sensed that He had tremendous authority, mixed with this wonderful love. I wanted to do what He told me to, although in another way I would have loved to stay where I was.

Then I made the journey back to my body. It was a strange experience as I re-entered my body – it wasn't very pleasant. I felt my spirit coming back into my body again, and it didn't feel very nice – I felt restricted, like being put into a box! And of course my head was very painful, due to the knock I had given it, which had caused me to lose consciousness. I was still lying there on the floor where I fell, but now my father and mother were also there, standing quietly, watching me. In spite of the fact that I had tried not to make a noise when going to the bathroom, and had in fact been very quiet, my mother had suddenly woken up, and had immediately sensed that something was wrong. She went around the house, trying to find out why she was feeling so disturbed, and then she found me, lying in the bathroom. She could not lift me on my own, so she called my father to come and help.

Dad came into the bathroom and was able to move me, so that I was lying on my back. But after that they themselves were unable to move. They wanted to call for an ambulance, but they both felt rooted to the spot. I am very close to my dad, and he told me afterwards that he sensed I was somewhere else, and they shouldn't attempt to move me. Although my parents at the time only had a formal interest in religion, they are now both born-again believers.

I have to admit that I didn't really want to move from that place, it had been so lovely to be in the Lord's presence, but of course I had to be moved, and I was helped back to bed by my parents. The wonderful thing was that the symptoms that I had been experiencing – fainting and passing of blood – stopped, and I quickly returned to good health. Since then, of course, I have been ill with other things, and on some occasions as I have prayed, the Lord has healed me instantly, in a way that could not be explained by any other means.

The intensity of the love that I felt from the Lord when I was in His presence, has given me a deep love for others. I feel their pain, and that is not always easy. It's like walking around with no shoes on at times! But you can't have an experience like that and remain unchanged.

Although I shared my experience with my parents, it was a long time before I started to tell anyone outside my family. I felt that people would not understand what I was saying, or that they would feel that I was crazy. But I now feel it's important to tell my story, because so many people just don't realize just how much God loves them – and they don't know that He loves before He judges, and that His judgement is always for our good. I know that people need to understand that there is a life beyond the body, and that our lives do not end at the grave.

10 HOWARD PITTMAN

On 3 August 1979, Howard Pittman, a Baptist minister for 35 years, died while on the operating table during surgery and had a near-death experience. After angels showed him the second and third Heaven, he was taken before the very throne of God where he was given a message to share with the world. Pittman preached 'Hell, fire and brimstone' for many years before his experience. During his near-death experience, his beliefs in the nature of God and Heaven were put to the test. The following excerpts are reprinted from his booklet Placebo *which documents his amazing experience.*

When the angels lifted my spirit from my body, they carried me immediately to the Second Heaven. We did not have to leave that hospital room in order to enter the Second Heaven. We entered there in that same room where my body was, just passing through a dimension wall. It is a wall which flesh cannot pass through, only spirit.

As we moved through that dimension wall into the Second Heaven, I found myself in an entirely different world, far different from anything I had ever imagined. This world was a place occupied by spirit beings as vast in number as the sands of the seashore. These beings were demons, or fallen angels, and were in thousands of different shapes and forms. Some of the forms were so morbid and revolting that I was almost at the point of nausea.

When I first arrived in the Second Heaven, I knew immediately in what direction I must go to reach the Third Heaven where God was. I don't know how I knew that, but I did. I also knew that if I was going to get my prayer answered, I was going to have to appear before God the Father in the Third Heaven. I was aware that I was travelling in that spirit world under the protection of the Holy Spirit, and that the angels who were escorting me were also moving about under the protection of the Holy Spirit.

As we moved about there in that world, I was greatly disappointed that my escort did not take me in the direction of the Third Heaven where God was. Instead, we moved in the opposite direction. As we moved from place to place in that world, I learned many things about demons.

I did things differently in the spirit realm than we do here in the physical world. For instance, we did not communicate with our mouths and ears, but rather, we communicated with our minds. It was like projecting our words on thought waves and receiving the answer the same way. Although I could still think to myself without projecting thought waves, I discovered that this really did not benefit me because the angels could read my mind.

I could hear different sounds in that world, but I did not hear with my ears. I heard with my mind, but I was still able to 'hear' those sounds. When we travelled, we travelled mostly at what I call the 'speed of thought'. When we travelled at the 'speed of thought', there was no sensation of movement. The angel would say where we were going and we were there. There were other times when we did not travel in that manner, and I was very much aware of movement while travelling. One of those times when I was aware of movement was when they brought me back into the physical world and allowed me to see the demons working here. We moved about here somewhat like floating on a cloud. Still, I had the sensation of movement.

When we started the tour of the Second Heaven, the angels began by showing me the different types of demons. Each demon was revealed to me in a form that indicated his area of expertise, and I soon discovered that there is no such thing as a 'general practitioner' in all the demon world. The demons are all experts in their fields. They have only one area of expertise which they do very well.

At one time during this tour of the Second Heaven, I watched the demons within their own related group and I experienced an awful feeling. It was an overwhelming, oppressive and morbid feeling. This feeling came to me shortly after I had entered the Second Heaven and I wondered what was causing it. It was at this time that I learned that the angel could read my mind because my guardian angel said to me, 'That feeling you are wondering about is caused by the fact that there is no love in this world.' The angel was telling me that in this Second Heaven there is not one bit of love! Wow! Can you imagine all of those demons serving a master they don't love and the master ruling over beings that he doesn't love? Worse than that, their companions are working together for an eternity and they do not even love each other.

I started reflecting on what our physical world, called the First Heaven, would be like without love. If God had not introduced His love here in our world, then we would be living in a no-love atmosphere like the Second Heaven. By God giving us His love, we are able to return that love and then love one another. Can you imagine what it would be like in your own home or your community if it was totally void of love?

My escort then told me that they wanted me to see demon activity in the outside world. I was then escorted outside the hospital directly through the brick wall into the streets of that city. I was amazed as I watched all the activity of the humans in the physical world. Going about their daily pursuit, they were completely unaware that they were being stalked by beings from the spirit world. I was totally flabbergasted as I watched, and horrified as I saw the demons in all shapes and forms as they moved at will among the humans.

The angels decided that I had seen enough of the demons at work in this physical world. I was taken back into the Second Heaven just by passing through the dividing, dimension wall. Once back inside the Second Heaven, my escort guided me in the direction of the Third Heaven and I was happy at last. After all, this was where I had wanted to go all the time. Even at this stage, my physical life was still my primary concern.

Suddenly we came to a most beautiful place. I know that I've already reported how terrible that Second Heaven was, so you can imagine how surprising it was to find anything beautiful over there. God would not allow me to retain the memory of why this place was so beautiful. I do remember that it was the most beautiful place I'd ever seen. This place looked like a tunnel, a roadway, a valley or some sort of highway. It had a most brilliant light all its own and was completely surrounded with an invisible shield. I knew that the invisible shield was the protection of the Holy Spirit.

Walking in this tunnel, or along that roadway, or valley, or whatever, were what appeared to be human beings. I asked my escort who they were. He told me, 'They are saints going home.' These were the departed spirits of Christians who had died on Earth and they were going home. Each of these saints was accompanied by at least one guardian angel and some had a whole host of angels with them. I wondered why some saints were accompanied by only one angel and others had many. I was watching as the saints passed through the way that all saints must take to go home. Here it was, the passageway from Earth to the Third Heaven.

Instead of allowing me to enter, the angel stationed me before the gates, slightly to one side. He instructed me to stay there and watch as the saints were permitted to enter into Heaven. As the saints were allowed into Heaven, I noticed a strange thing. They were permitted to enter only one at a time. No two were permitted to enter those gates at the same time. I wondered about this but it was never explained to me.

When the last of the 50 saints had entered into the Third Heaven, I started to enter but my escort stopped me. He told me that if I entered I could not come out and that I would have to stay there until the Father brought me back. The angels told me that all who enter the Third Heaven must remain there until brought back to this physical world by Christ Himself.

When the angel said I could not enter unless I stayed, I protested. 'But if I can't come out then my body will die! That will defeat my whole purpose!' was my emphatic rebuttal. Still my physical life, even at this point in time, was more important than anything else. My escort told me to stand to one side of the gates and present my case. He assured me that God would hear and answer my request

As I stood before the gates, the sense of joy, happiness and contentment radiated out from Heaven. I could feel the warmth it produced and as I stood there to plead my case, I could feel the awesome power of God.

Boldly I came before the throne and started out by reminding God what a great life of love, worship and sacrifice I had lived for Him. I told Him of all the works I had done, reminding Him that I had accepted Him when I was quite young and that I had served Him all my life for all these many years. I reminded Him that I was now in trouble and only He could help by granting me an extension of my physical life. God was totally silent while I spoke. When I had completed my request, I heard the real, audible voice of God as He answered me.

The sound of His voice came down on me from over the gates even before the words hit me. The tone of His anger knocked me on my face as God proceeded to tell me just what kind of life I had really lived. He told me what He really thought of me and even of others who did as I had. He pointed out that my faith was dead, that my works were not acceptable, and that I had laboured in vain. He told me that it was an abomination for me to live such a life and then dare call it a life of worship.

I could not believe He was talking to me in this manner! I had served Him for years! I thought I had lived a life pleasing to Him! As He was enumerating my wrongs, I was sure He had me confused with someone else. There was no strength left in me to even move, let alone protest, yet I was panicking within myself. No way could He be talking about me! I just could not believe that what He said was referring to me! All of these years I thought I was doing those works for God! Now He was telling me that what I did, I did for myself. Even as I preached and testified about the saving grace of Jesus Christ, I was doing that only for myself in order that my conscience might be soothed. In essence, my first love and first works were for myself. After *my* needs and wants were met or satisfied, in order to soothe my conscience I would set out to do the Lord's work. This made my priorities out of order and unacceptable. Actually, I had become my own false God.

Only now as I was here before Him being chastised did the meaning of certain portions of scripture become crystal clear to me. As God told me about my true motives, I could see plainly for the first time how my works were dead. Because God was displaying His wrath toward me, I could not stand, nor could I speak. No strength was left within me as I was nothing more than a wet rag lying there writhing in agony.

It needs to be stated that at no time while God was chastising me did He say I was not saved, nor did He say that my name was not in the Lamb's Book of Life. He never mentioned salvation to me at all but only spoke about the works produced through my life. He told me the type of life I lived was an unacceptable life for a true Christian. As He spoke to me of my dead works, He indicated that there are some people who are not saved but think they are.

When God was through with me the interview was over as suddenly as one would turn off a tap. I was not allowed to linger or even reflect on what God said. The angels immediately carried me away as if I were a wet rag having no strength in myself. Totally annihilated, I could not even gather my thoughts.

The angels carried me back through the Second Heaven, through the dimension wall, and into the hospital room where my body was lying. Not until I reached the bed upon which my body lay did I regain my composure. As I regained my composure, I vehemently protested, 'No! No!' I told the angels, 'God did not answer me! He did not say yes or no to my request! Please, oh please, take me back!' I pleaded with the angels.

Upon my arrival back before the Third Heaven, I was brought to the same place from which I had previously pleaded my case. Not nearly so bold this time, I remembered how God's wrath had floored me beforehand. Nevertheless, I had asked God for a favour and He had not answered. Wanting His answer no matter what it was, I timidly started pleading my case again.

This time God did not knock me down but let me talk. He did not talk to me in anger but started out answering me in a tone of pity. Before it was all over, He was speaking in sorrow.

Opening my plea by quoting scriptures to God, I began by telling Him all about Hezekiah. I told God that I figured out that Hezekiah was the 'good-old-boy' type, that the intentions of his heart were pure, but he seemed to be unable to translate those intentions into everyday living. Here I was, an insignificant nothing and the smallest creature in all His universe, bartering words with this great and awesome God who had created it all.

I said, 'Father, if You will grant this request, I promise You I will do better the next time.'

The Lord answered me, 'Howard Pittman, you have promised before.' He did not have to say another word. There they were, all the promises I had made to a Holy God in my entire past life. Not one of them remained whole. Somehow, some way, I had managed to break them all. With nothing left to say, no words in all my vocabulary, nowhere to go, I fell on my knees before Him. All I could say was 'Amen' to my own condemnation. I knew that if at that moment He would banish me into the pits of Hell, it would be just to say 'Amen' to my own condemnation.

At that moment He did not demand justice but showed me mercy. The scales fell from my eyes and my soul was suddenly filled with light. That powerful, awesome, all-consuming God was now not evident. There on that throne dealing with me was my *real* Father. He was no longer a distant God, but a real, genuine Father. The realization of His being my true Father and my best Friend came to me for the first time in my life. The wonderful relationship I had enjoyed with my physical father and the wonderful love we shared for each other was suddenly brought to mind yet magnified a thousandfold. For now I was with my real Father, the One who loved me so much that He left all of His creation to deal with me, the prodigal son.

For the first time in my life, I saw in my mind's eye who God really is. For the first time I met Him as He truly is, my real Father, my very best Friend. As the realization of who He is flooded my soul, great and painful sorrow also came. Sorrow came when I realized that through disobedience I had hurt my

Father. This realization and sorrow produced actual pain which was not just a guilt feeling but actual pain, similar to what one experiences in the flesh when one sustains a physical injury. At this point in time, He started dealing with me in sorrow and no longer did the tone of His voice express pity. Instead, the sound was of genuine sorrow. I suddenly realized that He was hurting too. God was hurting because I was hurting. Being a true and just God as He is, He had to allow me to suffer the pain and He could not lift it from me. Although He had to allow me to suffer the pain, He would not allow me to suffer it alone. God the Most High, the Most Supreme, the Creator of all, the Father of all would not let me suffer alone.

By this time I suddenly realized that my physical life was not so important after all. What I was really concerned about now was what my Father wanted. His will had suddenly become the first thing of my life and my physical life was no longer important. This is when He gave me back my physical life. Only when I reached a place that my life did not mean anything to me, did He give it back to me. Now that the prodigal son had returned, the Father could talk at last. He could tell me what my trip to Heaven was all about and that He had a message He wanted me to tell people on Earth.

I now repeat for you point by point the entire five-point message that God gave me to deliver to this world today.

1 For those who call themselves Christians, this is the Laodicean Church Age in which we live. A high majority of so-called Christians are, in fact, living a deceived life. They talk Jesus and play church, but do not live it. They claim to be Christians and then live like the Devil. They have bought the great lie from Satan who tells them that they are all right. He tells them that it is all right to go to church on Sunday and attend midweek services but as far as the rest of the time

is concerned, they are to get all they can out of life. As far as their Christian life is concerned, they believe they are comfortable and have need of nothing and as a result, they are only lukewarm Christians if Christians at all.

2 Satan is a *personal* devil.

3 To the whole world, this is Noah's second day. As it was in the days of Noah, so shall it be in the days of the coming of the Son of Man (Matthew 24:37). Man took no thought of what Noah was saying nor did man believe that anything was about to change. Notice the close parallel today. Mankind can see all the signs of the last days, yet man does not believe that anything will change. He does not believe in the impending coming of our Lord and he does not prepare to meet God.

4 For those who claim to be Christians, they are supposed to be ambassadors for Christ here on Earth. One cannot have any true witness or power in his life unless that one lives his Christian faith at all times, 24 hours a day, seven days a week. To be a true Christian one must live it, not just talk it. To honour God with your lips and not your heart is not acceptable. Those who accept the responsibility of teaching, preaching or any leadership role have much for which to answer.

5 God is now in the process of recruiting an army with which He will shake this old world one more time. By working through His soldiers, God will produce great miracles that will shake the established hierarchy of the so-called organized religion that is in this world today. These soldiers that God is now recruiting will demonstrate the power of God to a greater extent than did the disciples in the Pentecostal age. Now the recruitment has begun in earnest because God is about to perform the great miracles through His army that He promised us He would do in the Bible. John the Baptist

brought the spirit of Elijah into this world and he did not even know he had it. He denied it, but Jesus confessed that it was so. The purpose of that spirit was to make straight the paths of the coming of the Lord.

This story may be found on the Internet at the following address:
www.webmaster@near-death.com/pittman.html

Rev. Howard Pittman may be contacted at the following address:

Howard Pittman Ministries
PO Box 107
Foxworth
MS 39483-0107
USA

11 PAUL McWILLIAMS

Policeman Paul McWilliams never really gave a thought to where he would go when he died – until he was knocked down by a car in 1990. Suddenly he knew that Hell existed – because he had arrived there!

All policemen know that they have to be prepared for almost anything when they go on duty, especially if they are working in London, as I was on a particular Sunday in February 1990. Turning a corner just before midnight with my WPC colleague Linda, we spotted a fight taking place, and immediately went to break it up. As we stood on the zebra crossing, trying to restrain the people in dispute, a car came rushing towards us. It swerved to avoid hitting Linda, but in doing so hit me instead. That was the last thing I remember until I woke from a coma five weeks later.

When I came out of the coma I was told that I landed 25 metres from the car, having hit my head on the vehicle, causing a severe skull fracture. I then hit my head again as I landed on the pavement, causing multiple haemorrhages to the front of my brain and a massive haemorrhage at the back of the brain, which was just a hairline away from killing me outright. The first police officer who came along kneeled in the road to try and help me. My legs were severely fractured apart from where my leg had been protected by my police truncheon. It took the medics 13 hours to put me together again, inserting metalwork into my legs. It sounds like they would have had an easier job with Humpty Dumpty!

I'm told that during the five weeks that I was in a coma I clinically died a couple of times. Apparently I was not expected to live, due to the extent of my head injuries. It was said, however, that if I did manage to pull through the head injuries might cause severe brain damage and even blindness.

My life had been fairly uneventful up to this point. God had certainly not figured in it to any meaningful degree. Oh, my gran had got me to go to Sunday school occasionally when I was a young child, but it had made little impact. I hadn't picked up anything of significance about God or Christianity, and had in the end stopped going altogether. As I grew up my interests were focused on things like cars and money – I was as far away from God as one could possibly be, without of course being deliberately evil.

So it was interesting, to say the least, that during the time that I was in a coma I had a vision which would change my life, and my entire concept of Heaven and Hell.

I found myself standing in a place which I did not like one little bit. It was dark and cold, and I knew it was Hell. It was like being in a huge room, full of black oil – with a roof on it! I knew there was no way out. There were things moving under my feet, and I sensed that there was something coming to get me. I've heard people say they won't mind going to Hell, because they will be able to do all kinds of wicked things, with no restraint put upon them, but it was not like that at all. I experienced just about every horrific feeling one can think of, and worse. I could feel evil all around me, and I desperately wanted to get out of that awful place. I have to say that it's not a place where anyone would want to go. I could also hear muttering and murmuring going on, made by things that I could not see, but nevertheless feared.

Suddenly, for no apparent reason, I became aware of a faint glimmer of light above my head. Under normal circumstances I would never have noticed it, but because the place that I was in was so dark, any light at all, however dim, had an effect on the surroundings. I felt myself being pulled up and I was suddenly in a huge room with what looked like brown velvet on the walls. The back wall, however, was like a huge screen, in the sense that there was light coming from it. I could feel a warmth in the room which was such a huge contrast to the coldness I had just experienced. And the love and hope that I felt was in direct contrast to the hopelessness and despair that I had felt in that other place. As I gratefully started to adjust to the change in temperature, I saw a man walking towards me. I instinctively knew that He was Jesus, although He had never figured in my life at all, and I rarely, if ever, thought about Him. But now He was walking towards me, and I felt this incredible feeling of love coming from Him.

He was not like some of the pictures that I had seen in childhood books, when He was depicted with blond hair and fair skin. He was in fact quite dark-skinned, as indeed some modern-day Jews from the Nazareth area are. He was just a little shorter than me in stature, with a muscular body and a Jewish face, which interestingly had no spot or wrinkle upon it whatsoever. He was wearing a sort of beige or light brown coloured robe, which went down to His feet, and a simple belt around His waist. When He got within about 10 feet of me, it was as though I was engulfed inside a bubble containing a love which was a hundred times better than the love I had already started to experience. There was so much love there. Standing alongside me, He put His hand on my shoulder and also on my head injury that should have killed me (although I did not know that at the time, of course) and told me that He loved me and that I should not worry. I have since been told by my hairdresser that my head injury has healed so well there is no sign of where the massive fracture was.

Then he took me to what I can only describe as Paradise. It was wonderfully warm, like a summer's day. Everything was perfect, with not a blade out of place, not one chewed-up leaf – and the sky was perfectly blue. There was also a full rainbow going right across the sky. Although in one sense it was just like Earth, with trees, animals and water, it was far more beautiful than anything that I could adequately describe. At this point, I knew nothing about the Bible, and did not know that the book of Revelation talks about a new Heaven and a new Earth.

The next thing that I remember was falling or being catapulted through something very, very bright. It was like going down a well-lit motorway at night at a thousand miles an hour – but without any fear. Then I came into pain, and I woke up in my hospital bed, which of course was in intensive care. I don't know at what point I had the vision – whether it was at the beginning or middle of the five weeks I was in a coma, or whether it was right at the end. But when I woke up, I saw my sister sitting at the end of the bed, and said 'Hello', to prove to us both that I could think and see!

Many times my recovery has been described as a miracle. I had to retire from the police force, because of the high standard of physical fitness that they require, but I have experienced a wonderful recovery. Although I still cannot run or kneel, I can get around quite easily, in spite of the extensive damage that I sustained to my legs.

But far more amazing is that I now have a wonderful relationship with the resurrected Lord Jesus. He has changed my life completely, and the injuries I experienced are worth it all for what I have gained through knowing Him.

I can honestly thank the man who ran me over! I believe that before my accident happened on that Sunday in 1990 I was on my way to Hell – without ever realizing it. Now I *know* that I will go to Heaven when I die, and the wonderful thing is that everyone who invites Him into their heart can have that certain knowledge too.

12 VICKI

Vicki was born blind, her optic nerve having been completely destroyed at birth because of complications. Yet she appears to have seen during her near-death experience. Her story is a particularly clear instance of how near-death experiences in the blind can unfold in precisely the same way as do those of sighted persons. As you will see, apart from the fact that Vicki was not able to discern colour during her experience, her account of her near-death experience is absolutely indistinguishable from those with intact visual systems. The following is from Dr Ring's book Mindsight: Near-Death and Out-of-Body Experiences in the Blind, *and is used with permission.*

Vicki told Dr Ring that she found herself floating above her body in the emergency room of a hospital following an automobile accident. She was aware of being up near the ceiling watching a male doctor and a female nurse working on her body, which she viewed from her elevated position. Vicki has a clear recollection of how she came to the realization that this was her own body below her.

'I knew it was me ... I was pretty thin then. I was quite tall and thin at that point. And I recognized at first that it was a body, but I didn't even know that it was mine initially. Then I perceived that I was up on the ceiling, and I thought, "Well,

71

that's kind of weird. What am I doing up here?" I thought, "Well, this must be me. Am I dead?..." I just briefly saw this body, and ... I knew that it was mine because I wasn't in mine.'

In addition, she was able to note certain further identifying features indicating that the body she was observing was certainly her own: 'I think I was wearing the plain gold band on my right ring finger and my father's wedding ring next to it. But my wedding ring I definitely saw ... That was the one I noticed the most because it's most unusual. It has orange blossoms on the corners of it.'

There is something extremely remarkable and provocative about Vicki's recollection of these visual impressions, as a subsequent comment of hers implied. 'This was,' she said, 'the only time I could ever relate to seeing and to what light was, because I experienced it.'

She then related her out-of-body episode, which was very fast and fleeting. She found herself going up through the ceilings of the hospital until she was above the roof of the building itself, during which time she had a brief panoramic view of her surroundings. She felt very exhilarated during this ascension and enjoyed tremendously the freedom of movement she was experiencing. She also began to hear sublimely beautiful and exquisitely harmonious music akin to the sound of wind chimes.

With scarcely a noticeable transition, she then discovered she had been sucked head first into a tube and felt that she was being pulled up into it. The enclosure itself was dark, Vicki said, yet she was aware that she was moving toward light. As she reached the opening of the tube, the music that she had heard earlier seemed to be transformed into hymns and she then 'rolled out' to find herself lying on grass.

She was surrounded by trees and flowers and a vast number of people. She was in a place of tremendous light, and the light,

Vicki said, was something you could feel as well as see. Even the people she saw were bright. 'Everybody there was made of light. And I was made of light.' What the light conveyed was love. 'There was love everywhere. It was like love came from the grass, love came from the birds, love came from the trees.'

Vicki then becomes aware of specific persons she knew in life who are welcoming her to this place. There are five of them. Debby and Diane were Vicki's blind schoolmates, who had died years before, at the ages of 11 and six respectively. In life, they had both been profoundly retarded as well as blind, but here they appeared bright and beautiful, healthy and vitally alive. And no longer children, but, as Vicki phrased it, 'in their prime'. In addition, Vicki reports seeing two of her childhood care-takers, a couple named Mr and Mrs Zilk, both of whom had also previously died. Finally, there was Vicki's grandmother – who had essentially raised Vicki and who had died just two years before this incident. In these encounters, no actual words were exchanged, Vicki says, but only feelings – feelings of love and welcome.

In the midst of this rapture, Vicki was suddenly overcome with a sense of total knowledge: 'I had a feeling like I knew every-thing ... and like everything made sense. I just knew that this was where I would find the answers to all the questions about life, and about the planets, and about God, and about everything ... It's like the place was the knowing.'

As these revelations were unfolding, Vicki noticed that now next to her was a figure whose radiance was far greater than the illumination of any of the persons she had so far encountered. Immediately, she recognized this being to be Jesus. He greeted her tenderly, while she conveyed her excitement to Him about her new-found omniscience and her joy at being there with Him.

Telepathically, He communicated to her: 'Isn't it wonderful? Everything is beautiful here, and it fits together. And you'll find that. But you can't stay here now. It's not your time to be here yet and you have to go back.'

Vicki reacted, understandably enough, with extreme disappointment and protested vehemently, 'No, I want to stay with You.' But the Being reassured her that she would come back, but for now, she 'had to go back and learn and teach more about loving and forgiving'.

Still resistant, however, Vicki then learned that she also needed to go back to have her children. With that, Vicki, who was then childless but who 'desperately wanted' to have children *(and who has since given birth to three)* became almost eager to return and finally consented.

However, before Vicki could leave, the Being said to her, in these exact words, 'But first, watch this.'

And what Vicki then saw was 'everything from my birth' in a complete panoramic review of her life, and as she watched, the Being gently commented to help her understand the significance of her actions and their repercussions.

The last thing Vicki remembered, once the life review has been completed, were the words, 'You have to leave now.' Then she experienced 'a sickening thud' like a roller-coaster going backwards, and found herself back in her body.

This story is from *Mindsight: Near-Death and Out-of-Body Experiences in the Blind* by Kenneth Ring and Sharon Cooper (William James Center for Consciousness Studies, 1999), used with permission.

13 STAN EARLE

Motorbikes and young men seem to go together, giving a reason-
ably cheap and exciting form of mobility at a time in a male's life
when it's great to be on the move. But accidents can happen so
quickly, sometimes with devastating consequences.

I was born in 1958 into a loving, hardworking farming family.
I grew up around tractors, lorries – and motorbikes. Dad had
always driven a powerful motorbike so it was natural for me
to want one myself as soon as I was old enough. I passed my
motorbike test on my 17th birthday and then Dad surprised
me by giving me his own machine, a Triumph 500cc.

My mates also had motorbikes and we had a great time roar-
ing about. I loved riding fast with the rest of the gang.

One evening we were on our bikes travelling along Corbets
Tey Road in Upminster on our way to the house of a friend.
Two of my closest mates, Richard Burton and his passenger,
Andy Goff, pulled over to get some chips. I carried on for about
300 yards and then pulled over to get a Chinese takeaway. We
all must have pulled away at about the same time to continue
our short journey.

As I drove down the road with the bag of Chinese food held
between my teeth I decided to turn right into The Approach.
Witnesses said that I had signalled by hand to turn right and

then turned. However, unknown to me, my friends on their Kawasaki 500cc were about to overtake me at high speed. Instead they accidentally hit me side on, bending my motorcycle frame in half.

At the point of impact there were two realities. Those around at the moment of the accident saw the high-impact crash, saw our three bodies flying through the air to be hurtled down the road and then lying there, still and lifeless. But I experienced something entirely different. At the moment of impact, as if drawn by gravity, I fell immediately on to the road below me. I landed in the position of a sprinter, one foot back and one leg bent under my body with my arms straight, fingers touching the road surface. It's the position that sprinters take as they start a race, their rear leg against a starting block, ready to explode into action. This was the exact position I landed in at the point of impact.

From that position I immediately got up and walked over towards a big tree on the side of the road. I sat down under the tree with my legs crossed, as we used to do at our infant school. I was totally unaware that I was no longer in my physical body. I felt no pain, no fear, no anxiety, and I experienced absolute peace as I sat there under the tree.

Looking up the road I saw a motorbike in flames. I totally accepted the wonderful, Heavenly feeling without question. Although it was dusk when the accident occurred I was in a place of light. Nothing was troubling me whatsoever. It was a very beautiful experience. I was fully conscious of my surroundings and totally comfortable, sitting by the side of the road under the tree.

As I sat there watching the bike burn, I suddenly became aware of a huge dark cloud that filled the sky, coming down from above me, drawing my attention. I looked up and at the exact moment I looked up I heard a voice, gentle but so powerful, that filled the sky. The voice spoke directly to me. 'Do you want to take your crash helmet off?' he asked. My immediate reaction was a long, emphatic scream, 'Nooooooo!'

Immediately, I was back in my physical body watching the ambulance light going round. A policewoman said that as she approached my body to see if I was alive she heard my scream. The point I want you to grasp is that my scream started with me sitting under a tree in an entirely different place. The voice I heard sounded as the voice of God.

All of us had stickers on our crash helmets saying 'In case of accident, do not remove'. The question I had been asked, 'Do you want to take your crash helmet off?', was a very specific question, bringing me to immediate realization of my circumstances. I knew exactly what the question meant.

Once I was in hospital they realized I had broken my right arm and leg and had quite extensive skin loss from various parts of my body. Initially, I was absolutely certain that I had not broken anything. After all, I remembered quite clearly walking without any pain. As I walked I had a spring in my step and I had sat under the tree and watched the bike burn. The out-of-body experience was more real to me than the doctors telling me that I had broken my leg. At the time I would have laid all my money that they were wrong. However, they were not wrong. I ended up in plaster and spent a week in hospital.

My parents came to the hospital on the night of the accident, and were devastated. My dad came up behind me as I lay on a stretcher and gently told me that my two friends had died. What my dad told me I already knew. This knowledge had somehow been imparted to me to help me deal with the loss of my friends.

I had believed in God before the accident but obviously, after the accident, I was absolutely certain of the existence of Almighty God!

Although I recovered from my physical scars, my mental scars remained. I blamed myself for the death of my friends, even though that was illogical.

I only knew one Christian at the time, and she was my Aunt Betty. I thought she was a bit of a 'Bible basher' as she was always quoting scripture. Although deep down I knew that what she was saying was right, I always argued with her when I saw her, which was usually about once a year.

I had opened my own gym by the time 1979 came round, and I was married by the time I was 21. I competed drug free in two bodybuilding competitions. Then, after five years and eight months of natural drug-free training, and even though I had more than doubled my strength, I stupidly started taking steroids to compete against other drug users. By the time I was 27 I had entered my last competition, and my marriage was over.

I now had a new, more powerful motorbike, and on the surface I didn't have a care about anything, but underneath I was more and more concerned about the side effects of drug-taking on my mental and physical health. Then an injury to my left shoulder stopped me training completely. I decided to try more recreational drugs, believing that my incredibly strong will-power would prevent me from becoming addicted. After these two very crazy and destructive years I was just a shadow of my former self.

My shoulder was getting worse so I still could not train regularly, girls and drugs were my life and my life was one long party. My mum and dad wanted me to continue to run my own business, Stan's Gym, but I was hardly ever there. The drugs that I had always been against and the lifestyle my mum and dad had always warned me against, this was the life I had chosen. Thankfully I had a great mum and dad who never gave up on me. And Aunt Betty always took time to share her love of Jesus with me.

After a night out I came home in the early hours of a Sunday morning in April 1990. I lay in bed thinking about surgery. When I thought of surgery I had hope, I wanted the best surgeon and was willing to borrow money to pay. Then I suddenly thought, in despair, that it was going to take ages.

I wanted it fixed right then and I suddenly thought, 'God knows all about me, He created me!' Instantly I cried out to God from my heart in repentance, begging for my forgiveness from all my sins in Jesus' name. I then cried out, 'Lord Jesus, take my life!' and at that moment the peace of God came and Jesus gave me a brand new life. I was conscious of God's presence. God knew all about me. I felt transparent before God and received His love and forgiveness in Jesus' name.

I then prayed, asking for God to heal my shoulder so that I could do the things God knew I wanted to do – I wanted to do the will of God! After speaking truthfully to God, giving my life to Him, I went peacefully to sleep, knowing that my shoulder would be healed the next day. And to God's glory, it was healed.

After Jesus saved me I was initially frightened to tell anybody what God had done for me. I did not want to mess up such an important message. Then, seven months later, an old friend, Mark Cooper, came to see me and explained how he had also been saved by Jesus and given a new life. Mark, a new Christian himself, explained some of the Holy Scriptures to me so I could read them myself. Jesus promised his followers power from on high, the baptism of the Holy Spirit, to empower them to live the Christian life. I knew I needed the power Jesus had spoken of because I had told nobody except Mark Cooper that I had become a Christian.

Mark also warned me that the Devil would try to stop me reading the Bible every day and told me that Jesus said I needed to be baptized, immersed in water, in the name of the Father, the Son and the Holy Spirit. He was right on both counts. I had to persevere in reading the Bible, and when I did get baptized in the Holy Spirit I was filled with joy and peace like I had never experienced before. Now my greatest desire is to tell others how they too can find peace and eternal life through Jesus the Messiah.

For information about Stan Earle's ministry please write to:

Stan's Gym
9 Aveley Road
Upminster
Essex
RM14 2TN

14 CALVIN SUTCLIFFE

Nobody can predict the next 24 hours. Normally we go from one situation to the next without anything harmful happening to us. But just occasionally, through no fault of our own, we are put in mortal danger. That was certainly Calvin Sutcliffe's experience.

It was a Sunday evening, and I had been leading the worship in the evening service at the little evangelical church that I attended. I became involved with this particular fellowship after a move of the Holy Spirit some time before. When the service was over, most of us stayed around for a chat and a little bit of supper before going our separate ways. I was a single man of 33, and had come in my own van to the service. It was parked on the right-hand side of the road, facing towards the traffic under a street lamp, directly outside the house of the minister, Pastor Peter Whiteside.

I was putting my piano accordion into the rear of the van, as a car came down on the same side of the road as my van was parked and ploughed straight into the front of my van. Seconds before it happened Pastor Whiteside shouted out the warning, 'Jump, Calvin!' but it was too late. I was pushed underneath, immediately knocked unconscious, and then dragged 15 feet in a semi-circle while still trapped underneath my own vehicle. The impact was so severe that my van damaged the minister's car.

Meanwhile, I received brutal and serious damage to my body. Among other things I sustained a badly fractured skull and spinal injuries, and all the flesh was ripped off my right buttock. It was a cold evening, and I was wearing a fairly thick overcoat. Had I not been wearing the overcoat my injuries would have been far more severe, I am sure.

Help was obviously needed quickly, and two men, who just happened to be passing by, managed to lift the van from me. They must have been given superhuman strength to do such a thing. Meanwhile, someone had rung the ambulance, but I was 10 miles from an ambulance station in either direction, so it was quite some time before an ambulance came.

When the paramedics arrived, they couldn't even detect any breath when a mirror was put up against my mouth – and remember it was a cold winter's evening. I was put into the ambulance, and Pastor Whiteside was going to come with me. He was wearing only a shirt and thin cardigan over his upper body, and he started to shiver. Apart from the misty atmosphere there had been a frost that night, and the temperature was a few degrees below zero. The pastor felt a warm breeze come off the marshes, and when it hit him, he was as warm as toast, and he believed that it was God's power giving him an anointing of the Holy Spirit.

He got into the ambulance and decided to pray for me. After a while life began to come back to my body as he noticed my little finger starting to move. He said later that it seemed as though something entered my body at that point. I was taken to hospital.

I was in a coma for three days, but when I came round I was disappointed. I did not want to return. In one sense I had a lot to live for. I was still only 33, I was doing some school teaching and some ministry work too. But I knew that I had been to a place so wonderful, even though my memories from the beginning were vague, that I did not want to return.

I had experienced a wonderful, brilliant light, which had been at the end of a tunnel. I also remember feeling very warm and comfortable. I still have no idea where my spirit had been during those three days that I was in a coma, or when I had clinically died, but I was aware of returning from somewhere once I came out of the coma.

My terrible injuries were sorted out in an almost miraculous way. My fractured skull was left with just a slight indentation, which went away after a little while, and the spinal bruising also cleared after a short time. However, I was back on that same ward five weeks later, due to a thrombosis in my leg. A blood clot went to my lungs, putting my life in severe danger. It was as though I had to face death a second time. But the Lord had a plan in it all, because I was able to lead two people to Him. One was a Jewish lady who was seeking the Messiah and the other was a Roman Catholic priest. He had ministered in Kenya for 28 years as a missionary, but confessed as he was dying of cancer in the bed opposite that he didn't really know the Saviour as he should. So, in spite of the fact that I couldn't get out of bed to speak to them, I was able to talk to them about my relationship with Jesus, and that is why I am sure He allowed me to go back the second time.

15 SUSAN FINLAY

Long sunny days, picnics and swimming – what could be more idyllic? But when the swimmers are unsupervised children, having high jinks in the river, anything can happen. Susan Finlay was only seven when she suddenly realized that she was drowning – and that nobody had noticed what was happening to her.

My story happened way back in 1952, when I was just seven. Some people will remember that things were very different in those days as far as the care and supervision of children was concerned. Most kids were allowed to go and play with their friends all day long, without adults being present. That was certainly the case where I was brought up, a state of affairs that just could not be contemplated in the day and age in which we now live.

My childhood was spent in Oxford, and some days during the school holidays in the summer when the day promised to be warm and sunny I was allowed a picnic. It was often no more than some bread and butter and a bottle of water, but a picnic meant that I could use the whole day to swim and play with my friends on the banks of the River Thames without having to go home for food and drink. On Sundays I would go to Sunday school at St Michael's and All Angels in Summertown. Although I enjoyed it well enough, nothing from a spiritual point of view had had a major impact upon me at that stage – but then I was only seven!

We used to play near one of the bridges that span the river. Some of the older children, once they had got bored with splashing in the water, would climb on to the side of the bridge and jump off, trying to land on someone's head as they did so! It was never done in anger – more to prove one's skill and dexterity, I suppose. But all I wanted to do was to learn to swim. On the particular day in question I had brought a big black car tyre to the river with me, which I was using like a rubber ring. I carefully went back and forth from the bank to the deepest part of the river, feeling safe within my car tyre.

Then it happened. One of the children jumped off the bridge – and this time my head was the target! I was of course pushed under the water, and I immediately felt myself filling up. Water was pouring into my ears and my mouth, and as that happened I started talking to myself. I didn't feel panicky, strangely enough, but I found myself saying, 'Susan – you're dying!' I went to the bottom, filled up with water and then came to the surface. No one had noticed what was happening to me as there was so much laughter and shouting going on. Because no one had come to my aid I went down again, filled up some more, and came to the surface again. When I came to the surface for the third time I was near the bank, and I just got out of the water.

The odd thing was that nobody else was around. All the children had disappeared, and I was standing on a river bank on my own. I looked around in surprise. The trees looked wonderful, their leaves greener than I had ever noticed them before. And the grass! Why hadn't I ever noticed how perfect every blade was, the most wonderful green one could ever imagine as the blades shone in the brilliant sunshine? The sky too looked wonderful, the colour as perfect a blue as one could ever wish for.

But where was everyone? I started to wish that my mother was around to look after me. Everything looked wonderful, but it was odd being the only one around. I was of course no longer in Oxford, but had been given a tiny glance at what Heaven was like.

But the next thing that I knew, the river bank and the countryside had gone, and I was sat in a very large room with an enormous cinema-like screen on one wall. As I looked I began to see my whole life pass before me – which of course at the age of seven is not extensive – but everything was projected on to that screen, and I knew it was a summary of my life.

I was shown key moments during my brief period on Earth – what I had done, followed by what I should have done. Sometimes it was what I had said, followed by what I should have said. I didn't feel condemned, but I knew that what I was witnessing was true, that what was being said or shown was not something that I could or should argue against, because it was fair and right. I could hear a voice explaining things to me, but I did not see anyone or anything other than this huge screen. Then, as quickly as it had started, the whole thing was over, and the next thing I knew I was back on the river bank in Oxford, with my friends standing around me, pumping the river water out of me! After a while, I walked slowly back home, but did not tell my family what had happened, partly because I thought I might be stopped from going to the river again, and partly because it was just something I had experienced which couldn't really explain. But now I knew that the things that I was being told in Sunday school each week about Jesus and Heaven were true, and I started to listen with new interest and enthusiasm.

Life moved on, and I reached the age of 20. I'm not sure how much my drowning incident had affected me, but as I went through school I had found learning new things difficult. And there seemed to be a sort of imbalance in my body, which nobody really understood, but which I found really difficult to deal with.

Because of this imbalance I couldn't function normally. I couldn't stand normally. When I walked down the road, the road would appear to go down, and I felt that I was falling over. If I was in bed it felt as though I was falling backwards. It was very nasty, and I couldn't cope with it any more. One day, things just got too much and I ended up taking barbiturates together with some Valium and Librium tablets. I just wanted to die. I just wanted to be with Jesus. I spoke to the Lord and I repented in the best way I knew how – I had never done anything like this before, and I asked forgiveness for anything I had ever said or done that might have hurt anyone. Then I took all the tablets, and went to bed – I was still living with my parents at the time, and my brother lived in the house as well.

Five hours went by, with that evil cocktail of drugs doing their deadly work in my body. Then, just before my brother was due to come home, I was woken up, not violently, but very persistently, by someone, until I was fully awake. But then I realized that nobody else was in the house, and nobody could have gained access to the house, apart from my parents or my brother! Again it seemed that divine intervention had stopped me from dying. When my brother discovered me after I had been woken from my drugged state I was rushed to the hospital, and my body was pumped clean of all the harmful chemicals.

Then about six years ago, someone prayed for me for my balance problem, together with a spirit of fear that I had had for so long. Since then I have been able to live a normal life and enjoy a normal sleep pattern, something that I was never able to do up until then.

Why did I not die on at least two occasions? Well, only God really knows that, but I now try and tell as many as I can that Jesus loves them, and can help them through their most difficult times. And one of my three children is now a Christian minister, so he's involved in that work too.

Had I realized that I was getting a glimpse of Heaven when I drowned as a seven-year-old I'm sure I would have taken far more notice of what was around me. But I would have probably been scared too. In His wisdom God just let me think I was still in Oxford. Although it's a pretty part of the world, I now know that it's not a patch on where I know I'm going to live forever one day!

16 BILL WILSON

The following took place in the hospital room of Bill Wilson, the founder of Alcoholics Anonymous. This account is excerpted with permission from his biography, Bill W. *by Robert Thomsen.*

His hands clasped the footboard of the bed. But how? How? The alcohol had already killed his mind, his will, his spirit, and it was only a matter of time before it would kill his body. Yet at this moment, with the last vestige of pride, the last trade-off obstinacy crushed out of him, still he knew he wanted to live.

His fingers relaxed a little on the footboard, his arms slowly reached out and up. 'I want,' he said aloud. 'I want...'

Ever since infancy, they said, he'd been reaching out this way, arms up, fingers spread, and as far back as he could remember he'd been saying just that. But always before it had been an unfinished sentence. Now it had its ending. He wanted to live. He would do anything, anything to be allowed to go on living. 'Oh God,' he cried, and it was the sound not of a man, but of a trapped and crippled animal. 'If there is a God, show me, show me. Give me some sign.'

As he formed the words, in that very instant he was aware first of a light, a great white light that filled the room, then he suddenly seemed caught up in a kind of joy, an ecstasy such as he would never find words to describe. It was as though he were standing high on a mountain top and a strong clear wind blew against him, around him, through him – but it seemed a wind not of air, but of spirit – and as this happened he had the feeling that he was stepping into another world, a new world of consciousness, and everywhere now there was a wondrous feeling of a Presence which all his life he had been seeking. Nowhere had he ever felt so complete, so satisfied, so embraced.

This happened, and it happened as suddenly and as definitely as one may receive a shock from an electrode, or feel heat when a hand is placed close to a flame. Then when it passed, when the light slowly dimmed, and the ecstasy subsided (and whether this was a matter of minutes or much longer he never knew), he was beyond any reckoning of time – the sense of a Presence was still there about him, within him. And with it there was still another sense, a sense of rightness. No matter how wrong things seemed to be, they were as they were meant to be. There could be no doubt of ultimate order in the Universe.

Now, in place of the light, the exaltation, he was filled with a peace such as he had never known. From that time on Bill Wilson never took another drink.

This story may be found on the Internet at the following address:

www.pconline.com/~jsenear/bill.htm

17 DARREL YOUNG

Sometimes, in spite of the fact that we know we are ill, we ignore the signs, and the situation has to be taken in hand by others. It was Darrel Young's wife, Helen, who made an appointment for him to see the doctor. It was a good thing that she did. Nobody had realized just how sick he was. But in his hour of need, Jesus came to him in a special way.

My wife had been concerned about the state of my health for some time, so I wasn't really surprised when I learned that she had set up an appointment for me to see our family doctor. I was scheduled to see him on 16 October 1996. I have to say that when I heard what she had done, I had no intention of keeping that appointment, but as it happened I was not feeling well on that particular day, so I went along anyway. My wife warned the doctor ahead of time that I would probably not be very co-operative, and would possibly deny that I had a heart problem!

My wife requested that he should do an electrocardiogram, as he had done about a year earlier without finding anything. He referred me to a cardiologist for a stress test – maybe as a precautionary measure on his part. The stress test was performed by the cardiologist two days later on Friday, 18 October. After this test I was recommended to have a heart catheterization, which was done the following Monday morning. It was after this was performed that the doctors told me they wanted to perform heart surgery on me. The operation was scheduled for that Friday. There was nothing that I could do but agree to their proposals, although I asked if I could at least go home until Friday. But the doctors advised me to stay in hospital. So I was admitted to hospital and underwent preparations for the surgery they needed to perform.

Being a believer in God, and having witnessed several healings of others, I called for a prayer chain to be started. Several people from different denominations promised to pray for me. The day of my operation arrived, and my pastor came to visit me in hospital. He walked along beside me as I was being wheeled towards the operating theatre, and as he did so I took the opportunity to thank him for his part in organizing the prayer chain.

What I didn't say to him was that I had a strange sensation that I was going to die. I said to my wife that if I woke up and saw her face after the operation I would be happy – but if I woke up and saw the face of Jesus, I would also be happy – either way I would be happy. There were two promises God had made which had not yet come to pass.

Then, quite suddenly, before I was even in the operating theatre, I felt as though giant hands came down and wrung my heart like a wet dishcloth. The pain was indescribable, and I cried out, 'Jesus! God help me!' Again the pain came, and again I cried out. Then it came back for a third time. At that point I just asked the Lord to take me. Next thing I heard was one of the people working in the operating theatre say, 'His heart has arrested.'

Then it seemed that I was coming out of my body from where they had made an incision in my chest. And as I looked at the scene from where I now was, at the top of the room, near the ceiling, I heard someone else say, 'He has a hiatus hernia.'

The room then started to fill up with what at first glance appeared to be people but who I realized were in fact demons. They were having a great time, laughing and such because I had died. Then the most exciting and exhilarating thing happened. A hand came down and grasped my hand – my left hand. Immediately all the pain I had been experiencing ceased. Later, during our talk together, I thanked Him for stopping my pain. He said that He did not stop it – He took it, the same way He took all of my sins on the cross. I can remember thinking what an awesome power and love my Master possesses.

The robe that He was wearing was very beautiful, far more beautiful than I can describe. And the light coming from Him could never have been produced by a thousand powerful lights. The light coming from His face was not like the sunlight on Earth that would cause you to squint your eyes. I had always thought of His robe as being white, like the whitest cloth that one could imagine. But in fact what I saw was clear, pure white gold that flowed like cloth. Just as it says in Matthew 17:2 (NIV): 'His face shone like the sun, and His clothes became as white as the light.'

We walked out together through space, although it seemed as if we were moving with very little effort. However, I could tell that we were travelling at tremendous speed. Then I saw two sides of a beautiful walled city where they came together in one corner. There was a gate in the wall leading off to the left side. Leading up to the gate was a staircase of magnificent beauty. I felt it to be the Eastern Gate. It was made of pearl, just as I expected, but I didn't expect it to be covered by diamonds, rubies and other precious stones, with hinge straps of yellow gold. The staircase was made of yellow and white gold – and as I looked beyond it, I saw the most beautiful tinge of purple that I had ever seen. I wish I had words to describe it. The city was just sitting there in space, with no visible means of support, just like the Earth which I had left behind, which was now nowhere in sight.

We stopped on the fifth step and sat down. He sat me on his right knee, but at no time did He let go of my left hand.

I said, 'I didn't understand my dying before the two promises you made have been kept.' But He said, 'It's not over until I say it's over.' He was referring to the fact that He has power over life and death, which of course is true.

While we were sat together on the steps, lights were continually travelling from below to up above our heads, before bursting like fireworks all around us. I felt that they were very important, and it seemed as though I could almost hear them, but I could not make out what message they contained. Jesus explained that what I saw were prayers, coming up on my behalf from my prayer chain. I felt that there were far too many lights bursting around us for the people I knew who were praying for me, and He said that angels from all over creation were also praying for me. 'All prayers are heard by Me,' He said, 'and people ought to pray at all times.' It seemed as though, when I was in His presence, I had total knowledge about all things, but maybe that was because He kept hold of my hand.

Finally He said that it was time for me to go back. But then He added: 'But when I come to get you the next time I'll reach out and get your right hand, and you will be with Me forever.' We travelled back together in space. I was disappointed that I did not go into the Holy City, but I seemed to be satisfied with the reason that He gave me, although I can't remember now what it was.

The trip back seemed much faster than the trip out. He brought me back to the same spot in the ceiling where He had lifted me out. My body was still there, and was being frantically worked on by the doctors and nurses. The room was now totally filled shoulder to shoulder with angels, who were praising God. Just as the demons had looked like people, so did the angels that I could see. The demons did not have horns, and the angels did not have wings.

I dreaded going back into that body of mine, but I dreaded more leaving that love, joy and peace I had experienced with Jesus. I was in the operating theatre for several hours after I returned to my body. My wife Helen and our daughter came to see me afterwards. They had expected to see a terrible sight, based on what the surgeons had told them. I had a pump in my heart, two tubes in my throat, a tube in my neck – and a smile on my face! I later said to her, 'You'll never believe what happened to me.' As soon as I was able, I told her the full story. She made the remark that I would never be able to tell it again like I had just told it to her. I was just so full of emotion.

It's now my desire to tell as many people as I can about the love of Jesus for them. Because I know that when He returns to Earth again, which the Bible promises will happen, He is not coming to be born of a virgin, to suffer on a cross, and to shed His blood as a sacrifice for our sins. This He has already done. Next time He is coming as the Almighty Creator King in all His glory, and the time of grace that we currently live in will be no more. When He held my hand for six hours and 35 minutes Earth time, He showed me what total love and total peace is, and I will never be the same again.

For information on the ministry of Darrel R. Young please write to:

308 Cooper Drive
Charleston
WV 25302
USA

18 LAURA

Although Laura had always gone to church, it made little impact on her life. Then things started to go wrong – a broken marriage, a difficult delivery, and suddenly she knew that she needed God like she had never had before.

I am the daughter of an air force chaplain, so I was raised in the Church. I am also the second child, so I came with a streak of rebellion! I have always believed in a God but never really knew how to use His love for us all. I always stayed just outside the boundaries of being what I would call a bad kid – I would push the limits, but just not enough to be bad. Or so I thought! I married just after graduating from college and four years later had a child, then two years later I got a divorce. I don't want to go into the marriage but it took me to Al-Anon, where I found a God I could trust. This was a God who would help me in my daily life and I found a serenity I never had before – it taught me how to live, not die. I always believed in God because I was afraid not to – not because I wanted God's help, or trusted Him. I didn't attend church because it never really did anything for me. Notice I say *for me*.

Well, I found a new husband, and was married again, this time to someone who believed in God, not that it made much difference in our lives. We still never attended church, because it just wasn't something that meant that much to us. I did continue to go to Al-Anon, and tried to let God direct our lives. We counted on God but He still wasn't a big part of our lives. We both felt church was just a waste of time and to go wouldn't do anyone any good. Now I have to say I did feel a lot of guilt because I didn't take my daughter to church – I rationalized that I could teach her at home what she really needed to know about God. We started trying for a child and I even prayed about it, telling God I really wanted another one. Well, God finally granted me this wish and yet I carried a sense of unease for the next nine months. I felt like something was going to happen, and the closer it got to my due date the more uneasiness I felt. I never shared it with anyone, it was only a feeling and I couldn't explain it. I knew I would have surgery and I just figured it might be a Caesarean section.

One week before my due date, 22 January 1985, I came down with the flu and was very sick. My daughter had it and so did most of the town. In fact they closed down the school for a couple of days, so the kids could get away from each other with the hope they could stop the germs from spreading. The time got closer to deliver the baby and my due date came and went. I was glad it did because I was so sick. I knew that I couldn't go through the labour. Finally, at 9 p.m. one night we went to the hospital and I started my labour. Not much happened that night, so in the morning, around 10 a.m. on 4 February, the doctor broke my waters. I was running a fever through the whole thing and at 1.15 p.m. I gave birth to a 9lb 1oz baby boy. An X-ray showed that I had developed pneumonia and I was started on antibiotics. I still couldn't shake the bad feeling I had been carrying with me for the past months, and yet things seemed to be getting better. The doctor sent me home after five days, but during the night I started haemorrhaging, so back to the hospital we went.

As I lay in the emergency room I knew this was it – this was the bad feeling. But what did it mean? Well, I wouldn't stop bleeding, so they decided to take me to surgery and do a D and C. That is when I knew it, whatever it was, was going to happen. I was scared and couldn't stop what was going on. I have had surgery in the past, so I knew what to expect when you wake up. After the surgery was over I felt myself starting to come round but knew it would be some time till the drowsiness completely wore off. I was so relieved I had made it and hadn't died. Just at that very moment I felt my heart flutter and the drowsiness went away.

My mind was so clear and yet I wasn't awake. That threw me, because you don't shake off the drowsiness that fast from anaesthesia and yet I did. I also knew something was happening to my heart and then I realized I was dying. I felt myself lift from the heaviness of my body and at that point I also heard my doctor yell my name.

I found myself in a grey, cloudlike mass and could tell someone was with me. I turned toward him and said, 'God, I can't go now, I have a baby to take care of.' I have no proof it was God or who it was and I never asked. Just that quickly I felt myself being sucked back down and the heaviness of my body return. I tried to fight it and realized I had no control over what was happening. I was told to just let go. So there you have it! I have never had an experience so real in my life and even today when I think of it, it is just like it happened to me yesterday. But now that I had had a near-death experience, I lived in fear for the next year that God would take me again. After all, it was so easy to do and I was selfish – I wanted to stay. I was also a little mad God hadn't given me the big near-death experiences I had read about. People told me it wasn't real and yet I knew it was, so I stopped talking about it.

On my son's first birthday I realized I was living in fear and not enjoying what God had let me come back to. So I started to change my life. Church became an important part of my life and I started becoming involved. But there was a part of my near-death experience I didn't deal with, not for the next several years. I wouldn't talk about it or face it. I just shrugged it off and yet I knew it was also real. After I re-entered my body, I went into a coma. To this day I still don't know how long for and don't really care. But that is where the rest of my near-death experience took place, so it is just as important to me as the out-of-body part.

I found myself in front of a group of men-lights. It was so strange to me and they were asking me questions about my life. I don't remember what I told them but I do remember the feeling it was giving me. I was experiencing the most horrible guilt I had ever known. I wanted to run and yet I remember thinking, I can't believe telling these people all this stuff. I knew that it was things that I had hidden deep inside and thought no one would ever find out. Well, it wasn't hidden from God and I couldn't hide. The next thing I remember was trying to wake up. I knew it was going to be hard to do but I had to try. I couldn't get my body to wake up and yet my brain was awake, so I started trying. Slowly I woke up and started crying, and did so over and over for some time.

The guilt didn't leave me and so I shoved it aside with the hope that it would go away. I still don't know what I told them. The way I have to look at it is that if I knew all I did wrong in the past, I could have come back and changed those things. The way it was left I had to come back and search and find the truth in my life and change whatever I found to be wrong. I now rely on God and the Holy Spirit to show me the truth and help me to change the things in my life I need to change. This experience didn't make me a saint, but it did give me the power to change my life and a belief in a God I can depend on in everything I do. I have also come to understand that God gives us all different experiences so we can witness in different ways.

I have shared this experience and taught my children the need for God to be utmost in our lives. My daughter has gone through the sudden death of her first boyfriend and God has got her through that. Today she is a student at a Christian college and wants to do God's work when she graduates. My son, who will be 13 on 4 February, is a very strong Christian, who wants to be and is very active in our church. My husband and I, even though we have had our difficulties, are also both active in the church. I am proud of him for finding God; he has done so without a near-death experience as I was privileged to have. I just hope my experience can touch other people so they can do God's work without such an experience.

I feel the people who do trust and follow God without such experiences are so much stronger and will benefit when it is their time to leave this Earth.

This story may be found on the Internet at the following address:

www.pconline.com/~jsenear/laura.htm

19 DAVID PAIN

*You would expect most young men of 19 to be fit and healthy –
and most of them are. But accidents can happen so quickly, and
can sometimes be life-threatening.*

I had always enjoyed good health and a happy life. My home
life was happy. My mother originally came from Greece, and
was a real character. She used to send me along to Sunday
school each week, and there has never been a time when I did-
n't believe in God.

By the time I was 17 I had a job working for a friend in a
bakery in London. The work was going well. In fact, we had
more work than we could handle, and I was detailed to help on
a rush job that had to be completed by the morning. So, even
though I had worked a full shift that day, I then started work
again throughout the night.

About one o'clock in the dead of night, there was an accident. Part of the machinery that I was helping to dismantle fell
down and got caught in my shoulder. I was young and healthy,
and needed to get on with the job in hand, so I ignored what
had happened, got a bit of rag, put it over the wound, and for-
got all about it.

About six months later I was working in Oxford, on the
Banbury Road, doing some sub-contracting painting. I needed

to keep working on this particular job in order to make it pay, so when I began to realize that my left shoulder was starting to feel uncomfortable, I ignored it and hoped that the increasing discomfort would ease off. But that was not the way things turned out. In fact, by the end of the day the whole of my arm was swollen, as well as one side of my face.

When I got up the next day the swelling was still there. I began to feel a little concerned, so I decided to get it checked out at one of the several hospitals in Oxford. A friend had come to visit, so we walked to one of the hospitals through the beautiful University Parks.

When we got to the hospital we headed for the accident and emergency department. As we were stood in the queue waiting to give my name and why I was there, I noticed one of the nurses looking at me in a strange way. The next thing I knew that same nurse had gone away and reappeared with a stretcher, and suggested that I got on to it – this was before I had even been examined! Rather taken aback, I did what I was told, and then I was wheeled into accident and emergency. Doctors were summoned, and started to take a look at me. My friend and I kept giving each other quizzical glances – we had no idea what was going on, or why I was the centre of so much interest. Then I heard one of the doctors speaking to someone on the phone. 'This is an emergency – it looks like it's a thrombosis.' I lay there thinking, 'That sounds bad – I wonder who they're talking about,' not having a clue that they were actually talking about me! My friend had heard what the doctor had said, and he leaned over to me and said, 'I think they're talking about you.'

Things happened very quickly after that. They ran a whole series of tests, including putting a dye into my bloodstream, which confirmed their suspicions that they were dealing with a major thrombosis. But something else had happened to me. I was suddenly aware that although my friend was still with me, another presence was with me as well. I find it difficult to explain, but I know from that point on, all the stress and worry of the situation just disappeared, and I felt totally calm and at peace, in the midst of this activity that I was the centre of. It was as sudden as somebody turning a light on – or off.

The next thing I knew, I was experiencing an acceleration of my spirit. I had no idea what was happening to me, but then I stopped quite suddenly – it was like someone had put the brakes on when I was travelling at 50 miles an hour. My journey had taken me from my bed, into a place that was absolutely huge – I mean, it was colossal. And the brightness was remarkable – brighter than the sunniest day that you could ever wish for. I realized that three people were standing in front of me. One of them, the one in the middle of the group, started to speak. It wasn't an audible voice, but one I could hear nevertheless through my spirit. What was distinctive about this voice was its authority – I knew it would not have been right to argue or cross what it was saying.

What I heard the voice say was: 'It is not yet your time. You will have to go back.' When I came round, the doctors couldn't get over the fact that I was so calm, and not at all stressed by the things I had experienced. It was touch and go whether I would survive for a while, which was a shock to me and my family, especially as up until that point I had never suffered any real health problems. Looking back, I feel that had it been my time to die at that point, the acceleration that I experienced which took me into that room would have continued, and I would have ended up in Heaven. But as it was, because it wasn't God's plan for me to die at that point, the three that I encountered – and I have to be honest and say that I have no idea who they were – were there to stop me going any further.

I didn't have to stay in hospital for long, as it turned out. Once the various drugs were administered to thin the blood, the immediate danger passed. But my attitude to dying has changed. I have no worries about that. In fact people remark on my upbeat attitude towards life in general. I think that it's because I have experienced what it is like to die – but I know that there is nothing to fear if we have a relationship with the Lord.

20 ELIZABETH ATKINSON

Libby Atkinson had been exposed to the Christian message from the time she was born – her father was a Christian minister looking after a church of over 200 people. But as a six-year-old girl, it seemed that the God her dad talked about was loving one minute and angry the next. She was to find that He was far more loving than she could imagine. But before that she had to face a very traumatic situation.

Although my father was a Christian minister, an occupation not known for its high earning power, I was brought up in a very large house. He purchased it from ICI at a knock-down price. It had 46 rooms, and stood in two and a half acres of ground. In order to keep it running, my dad had single young men living there, who would normally have found it difficult to find accommodation. They helped maintain the building and do some of the gardening, and paid very little rent. Many of them became Christians, and ended up going into the Christian ministry.

But I was confused about the God that my dad talked about. It seemed that one minute He could be angry, and the next loving. Where was the consistency in that? I sat through a lot of 'Hell and damnation' preaching when I was young, which scared me. Mum had a lady who came round to help keep the house clean. The way she loved Jesus really impressed me. She just went around the house praising the Lord. But after six months, she never came any more. I heard that she had died, and I didn't understand why God allowed that to happen.

Meanwhile, getting a chance to spend time with Dad was near impossible – after the members of the church, the 15 lodgers and the rest of the family had had their time with him, there was little left for me. I also became aware of the fact that I had a fear of death, although I had no idea at the time where that had come from. It was years later that I discovered, quite by chance, that one of my parents' relatives had been involved in the occult in quite a big way.

When I was about six, we went on a church house party to Eastbourne. There was always something about me that wanted to help and rescue people and things – it was just part of my nature. So, during a game of volleyball on the beach, when the ball went into the sea, it seemed the natural thing for me to do was to go and wade in after it.

There is a stream that runs through the sea at Eastbourne – it's easily seen when the tide is out. This causes strong under-currents and one has to be very careful, even in comparatively shallow water. The ball seemed to move out so quickly, and I followed as fast as I could. Before I knew it, I was having to stand on tiptoe, to keep the water from going up my nose. It was at that point that I knew I had to decide whether to go deeper – I still hadn't got the ball – or turn round. Did I want to turn round? Or did I just want to be with Jesus? I decided that I had had enough, and that to be in Jesus' company for ever would be wonderful, and I allowed myself to go even further into the sea.

At that point, I saw all my life flash before me – not that I had lived much of a life as a six-year-old – but it was all very graphic. It was then that I remember coming out of my body, and suddenly as I looked down I could see the sea, and this thing flopping around in the water. Then I realized it was my body! Just at that point, everything went black. What had happened was that my dad had seen I was getting into difficulties, and had waded in to get me. I know I should have felt grateful – but I didn't. For those few minutes, I had appreciated the absolute peace that I felt, and being without the need to fight things all the time.

By the time I was 12 I pestered my parents to allow me to fly. They couldn't take me anywhere – they were too busy – but they persuaded a family to take me with them on their annual holiday. This family had two boys, who had a passion for creepy-crawlies – and they thought it was great fun to put those dreadful things in my bed each night! Our travels had taken us to a little village near Interlaken. I was about halfway through a six-week break away from my family, and I was terribly homesick. I spent most of my time on my bed, crying. One afternoon, I felt so upset, and was crying again when I suddenly felt a hand on my back. At the same time I heard a voice say, 'Libby, didn't I tell you that I would never leave you or forsake you?' I looked to my side, and stood there was this extremely tall being, surrounded by light. I only saw Him from the waist down, but He must have been very tall, when I think of how high His waist was from the floor of the room. I remember looking at the beautiful golden girdle that He had around His waist. But the light was so bright, it was almost like someone was shining a light in my face. I decided not to tell anyone what I had seen, but from then on I imagined Him around me, and it helped me to cope much better than I had been doing before.

By the time I reached the age of 18, I felt I ought to get baptized to please my father, which is just about the worst reason for getting baptized. I felt guilty as the baptismal service began, because I knew I was doing it for all the wrong reasons, and I knew most of the church knew that too.

But as I stood in the baptistery I saw what looked like a grey wall come down, which separated me from the congregation. Now I could no longer see the people in the church, which made me feel a little better. Then, just after I had been baptized, I saw Jesus standing at the edge of the baptistery waiting for me to come out. He said, 'Come, my child, and enter into all that I have prepared for you.' He took my hand and led me to the door that I had to go through to get changed. Then, as I got to the door, He just disappeared.

The years rolled on, and I had married. Life was going along quite nicely until I became ill through a viral infection. My husband had cooked two boiled eggs for me to eat. I had lost my appetite and was in need of some nourishment. He even chopped the tops off for me, but I was just too weak to dig out the egg from the shell. I desperation I cried out, 'God, you've just got to help me!' Moments later there was a knock on the door. I could hear a woman's voice I did not recognize talking to my husband. 'Is there a woman called Libby living here?' I heard her say. My husband was obviously cautious about saying too much to a stranger, but I called out and told him to invite her in. The stranger then told us her story.

She had been praying, and the Lord told her that He wanted her to go to the house of a woman called Libby. He gave her my address and told her what she had to take with her: complex vitamin B tablets for building up strength, Complan, because I had not been eating, and some teaching tapes, for building me up spiritually. He also told her to put a day aside, as I had lots of ironing I needed to catch up on! She had heard correctly on each key issue – even getting the correct address from the Lord!

This was the kind of God that I was interested in. A practical God, who loved and cared for mankind, and wanted to help and heal. I started to read my Bible afresh, and began to notice that the God talked about in that book was very different from the one I had heard about for so long as a child. He had proved His love for me on different occasions over the years, and I could doubt Him no longer. Since then, His care, protection and deliverance has been a part of my life, and I love to tell others what He means to me.

21 WAYNE SHAW

Wayne Shaw was not greatly concerned when he started to get a sore throat – he realized that he had been smoking too much, due to the stress he had been under. What he didn't realize was that he was about to have a massive heart attack, taking away his life, but also giving him a glimpse of his Maker.

Looking back, my problems started through difficulties I was having at work. I was employed by a telecommunications company, and started to have problems with my health which were related to stress. I got to the point where I was waking up in the middle of the night, sweating through the panic attacks that I began to experience. My doctor advised that I take some time off work. The stress started to make me feel depressed, and then during the second week that I was off work my father was taken into hospital, and was diagnosed as having cancer. Within three weeks he was dead. That increased my depression, causing me to take yet more time off work.

I was still off work two months later – but I knew that I needed to get out of the house, and start to get busy again. I offered to help a friend of mine called Glyn, who was working on a road gang in Stroud. In spite of the fact that it was early June, the work wasn't going very well when I arrived, because of the rainy weather, and I ended up standing around a lot, chatting and smoking numerous cigarettes. Then, around about 11 o'clock, I started to get a really bad throat, which I thought was related to smoking. Someone suggested that I take in some fluids, but that didn't work – I felt hoarse and dehydrated. I ended up in a pick up truck, waiting for Glyn. By then my teeth had started to ache, and a little while later I began to get indigestion-type pains in my chest, before being violently sick. He now realized that there was something quite seriously wrong with me.

I noticed some houses in the distance, and wondered if someone in one of the houses would be able to assist me to get some medical attention. It was becoming clear to me that maybe I didn't need a doctor so much as a hospital. Sweat started to pour off me when I just turned the ignition key. I wanted to be sick again, and had a terrible pain in my elbows.

After about 10 minutes, but what seemed like a lifetime, I saw a vehicle with yellow flashing lights coming towards me. It was the foreman who had left me in order to get Glyn to drive me home.

I was now feeling pain in every part of my body. It was too painful even to wear my seat belt. They were counting the miles as we went along, to try and keep my spirits up, and although I had no experience of God, I was praying that He would help me. It was 30 miles to Cirencester, and I was aware of every mile. I was awake, but not really taking things in – it was as though I was slipping or collapsing. But that wasn't the worst of my problems. I felt as though there were a herd of elephants standing on my chest, yet strangely enough at this point the possibility of having a heart attack had not crossed my mind.

I saw road signs to Cirencester, and suggested to the guy sitting next to me that we ought to go straight to the hospital. I now had a terrific headache, and it was all I could do to hold myself together.

On arrival I went straight to Casualty. I stood at the desk – and promptly collapsed. I was put on a stretcher, and a doctor said that he was going to give me morphine. I immediately thought I had cancer, because my mother always said after my father was admitted to the hospital and was put on morphine that 'this is the beginning of the end'. Then I heard someone say 'He's having a heart attack,' and it actually came as a relief to hear that! The medics wired me up to some machines and whisked me off to Cheltenham by ambulance.

I was aware of the ambulance rushing along the roads and an ambulance man, holding my hand, trying to give me some comfort. But I felt terrible. I was in emotional turmoil, and I felt very sorry and upset about what was happening to me. I must have lost consciousness, because the next thing I remember was being in a lift in a Cheltenham hospital. Soon I was put on a course of morphine, which made me feel high for about three days. By the time I was fully conscious again, my mother, sister and elder brother had arrived from South Wales. My mother wanted to know how I felt and I said, 'If they can sort my throat out I'll be happy.'

After three days I was moved to an outside bed in the ward, indicating that I was starting to recover. But what we patients could and could not do was strictly monitored, because the staff didn't want us to get too excited about anything. Therefore we couldn't watch TV, but we were allowed to hear certain programmes through headphones. For most of the day I had worked on a huge jigsaw with a lady called June Harris. It had taken a lot of my energy, but I was pleased that I had finally completed it. I sat on my bed. I was waiting for the comedy programme *Porridge* to start after the nine o'clock news, but as I picked up the headphones to listen to it, I collapsed.

I was aware of keeling over very quickly. I felt myself going forward, then all of a sudden I was unconscious. I was in total and utter darkness. It was as though I'd been dropped off the edge of the Earth. I had no feeling and therefore no pain. I don't know how long I was like that, but after a while it was as though I was being taken somewhere. I appeared to be in a void – there but not there – it's very difficult to describe. I remember shouting that I didn't want to be there. I started shouting, 'No, no, no, please God, no,' and giving out a long-drawn-out scream.

Then a light appeared in the corner. It completely lit up the left-hand side of me. The scene immediately changed from total blackness to light, which seemed to be coming from a kind of archway. Then I saw a figure with His hands outstretched. But He wasn't calling me. The light was now so bright that I couldn't see colours. All I could see was black and white. He was brilliant white with a crown on His head. I also noticed that He was wearing a cloak. I couldn't see His feet, or any of His facial expressions because of the brightness, which was whiter than anything I'd ever seen before. But it was not a blinding light, because I could see into it.

It was as though the figure came out of the light, and did not have a definite outline that could be drawn. The shape was obviously not the figure of a young person. So there I was, still screaming and yelling at the situation that I was in. I was very afraid. I believed the figure before me was God and that I was going to die. In fact, at the back of my mind I knew that I was already dead. You have to remember that at this point I was not a Christian, but looking back I believe that had I been a Christian I would have gone to be with the Lord at that point. So there I was, unable to take my eyes off this figure, who was strangely beautiful, and who started to have a calming effect on me.

Then I started to have glimpses of my body in the hospital again – I went from seeing myself to going back into the blackness three or four times. Suddenly I was back in my body again.

This time I remember looking up at the ceiling and having a great feeling of relief and release. I now felt calm. I started to tell the nurse that I had seen a king. That was the best way I could describe what I had seen. 'Well, you must have seen something,' she said with feeling, 'look at my arms!' I could actually see a handprint on her arm where I had gripped her. Although no one doubted that I had seen something, no one seemed particularly interested either.

I now felt totally relaxed. I had been resuscitated with electrodes and my chest was black. I didn't have any pain when I initially came round, but I did when the bruising started to come out. It seemed to me that my heart had stopped for about 20 minutes, but I'm told that it couldn't have been more than three or my brain would have been damaged.

I now had so many questions buzzing in my mind. Why had I seen the figure? What was I supposed to think about it all? I told my mother and my girlfriend, but when they took a lighthearted attitude towards it, I thought it best not to mention it again.

Then, on the very last day of my rehabilitation classes, I met a Christian called Howard Tarledge. Over a period of time I was able to tell him what I had experienced, and he said that he felt sure I had met with God. A few weeks later he invited me to go to a meeting where the New Zealander Ian McCormack was speaking, and it was through his ministry that I finally became a Christian.

After I had committed my life to the Lord, I felt I had to see my mother and tell her what had happened. When she heard what I had to say she went upstairs, but reappeared after a few minutes with a Bible in her hand. 'I've been saving this for you since my mother died,' she said. It was then I discovered that my grandmother was a Christian, and had no doubt often prayed for my salvation during her lifetime. I know that God brought me back from the dead, and now all I want to do is to live for Him.

22 LINDA SWAIN

Bringing a child into the world should be one of the most joyful and fulfilling times of anyone's life, but for Linda Swain on two occasions it brought stress and a threat to her own life. Yet God used those times to let Linda experience His love in a way that has stayed with her since.

I came from a broken home, and from the age of 12 upwards I was virtually on my own. Before my parents split up I went to church most Sundays, and loved to go, even though I didn't understand much that was going on. After the break-up, however, an aunt came to look after me and my brother for a while, and I was unable to go to church. I remember making a promise to God that I would be a secret believer.

By the time I was 21 I was pregnant with my first child. I was very ignorant about how the human female body works. When I started to miscarry I didn't know what was going on, and I didn't have anyone to ask about that sort of thing. By the time I did manage to pluck up courage to ask someone, the situation was such that I needed urgent medical care. I was taken to hospital. I was treated with bed rest, but after two days under observation I was taken up to the operating theatre. Suddenly I was aware of a white light in front of me, and I wondered why it was there. It seemed to have magnetic qualities, and I felt drawn towards it. The next thing I knew, I was in a room, with people moving about. I felt warm, comfortable and there was a sensation of kindness all around me. I felt as though I really did belong there, and, after all the trauma of the last few days, not to mention the last few years, I did not want to go back to where I had come.

Then to my surprise, an older gentleman came up to me. He was dressed in white, and he started to tell me off! He said that I couldn't stay where I was, but I had to go back. He was very insistent, but in such a loving way that I found it difficult not to agree. But I said my problem was that I never learned from mistakes that I made. He obviously won the argument because the next thing that I knew I was back in the operating theatre, having lost the baby.

A few years after this first experience I married, and in time we had a child. Thankfully the pregnancy and delivery were perfectly normal. However, problems started to arise when I was pregnant with my third child. I was taken into hospital again, and during a very difficult labour, I collapsed and became unconscious. Unlike the first time, I was not aware of being drawn anywhere. This time it was if I had suddenly arrived in this place where everything was white! The buildings were like prisms, so it was almost a jewel-like place, with everything shimmering. My labour had been so bad, I was convinced that I had already lost my baby, so I said to the first person that I saw, 'I'm looking for my baby.' Their reply took me by surprise. 'Nobody owns children here – they belong to everybody.' I thought it was a weird thing to say, not knowing at the time where I was. The man who had spoken to me was a kind of elder, dressed in white, as indeed was everyone else. Everyone knew who I was, and nobody seemed surprised that I was there. I was intrigued by this statement that nobody owned any child, and was then told that husband-and-wife relationships were not the same as they were on Earth, which again left me feeling confused.

I was allowed to wander around, and I started looking for flowers. I must have mentioned this to someone because they said, 'We can show you. We can show you anything you want – if you want to see it, we can make it happen,' and then before my eyes appeared this array of the most beautiful snowdrops, a flower that I have always loved. Just like the time before, I felt warm, comfortable and welcomed. I knew by now, of course, that I was in an extraordinary place, and I wandered around and had another conversation with these elders. I questioned the things that I saw, and each time they explained why things were as they were there. But then they said that I couldn't stay – I had to go back. I was not ready to stay there – yet. I remember trotting out my former argument that I did not learn from my mistakes, so there was no point in returning. They told me that I would learn, and that there was a work for me to do when I returned, but it would all happen within the course of time. They said that I needed to learn patience, and within time it would come. Then at that point I saw another figure, whom I took to be Jesus. He too was dressed in white, and there was a light around Him, which made it difficult for me to see exactly what He looked like. He confirmed that I would need to go back to Earth, but added that He would always be there for me, and that I would know that He was there. I never felt afraid during the time I was speaking to Him.

I got the impression there was a kind of hierarchy or order, with each person assigned their own work. Strangely enough I wasn't disappointed when I was told that I had to go back, but reassured, because I had been told that there was work for me to do.

The next thing that I knew I was back in the ward, with the nurses around me, trying to bring me round. When I realized that I was back on Earth, I started to feel upset, because I thought my baby had died. I had looked at the bottom of the bed, where they used to put the babies in those days, and there was no cot there, so I assumed the worst. I must have said something to that effect, because one of the nurses said, 'No, the baby's not dead, she's screaming for her feed in the baby unit.' So I was then taken to see my new baby, and to give her a feed.

Since then I have become more interested in reading the Bible, going to church, going to women's meetings and retreats, anything in fact that gives me more information and insight into how God works. I know that some people will be sceptical about what I have said, but I'm not out to try and prove anything, I just want to put on record what I experienced. What people make of it is up to them. I know that since my two experiences my attitude to death has changed. I used to have an enormous fear of death, although I don't know where it came from. I realized when my father died that the fear had gone. I went to see him for the last time in the chapel of rest. After I had sat with him for a while, and read a little of the Bible that was in the room, I went to kiss him, and it suddenly came to me that it was no longer my father lying there, but just a shell – he had already gone. And I know, apart from the trust I put in the verses in the Bible, that I will go once again to Heaven when I die, because I was told that was where I am ultimately going to be.

I have to say that I still don't know specifically what I should be doing – what my designated job is. But I remember I was told that I needed to have patience, and that I would be shown ultimately what it would be. I know in my own mind that I felt it important to let the children grow up before I launched into any major work, especially given my own difficult adolescence, so maybe that time is now approaching.

One thing I have noticed since my experiences is that I have confidence in praying for things to happen. Even when things seem to be really difficult, I seem to be able to pray and see situations turn around. Maybe that's just the Lord's way of saying that He is keeping His promise to be with me and watching over the things I do.

23 ANN PARNELL

Most routine operations turn out to be just that – routine. But occasionally things happen that nobody anticipates. This was Ann Parnell's experience – but Jesus was there, giving her the help that she needed at exactly the right time.

'We'll be praying for you,' friends assured me when I told them that I was going into hospital for a routine gall bladder operation. I appreciated their concern, but had not given a lot of thought to what I would be going through – I was now 50, had been a Christian since the age of seven, and had no fear of hospitals.

Everything went according to plan until I started to come round from the operation. I had been taken back to my room with tubes and a drip attached to me, and all I wanted was to be left alone and allowed to sleep. The nursing staff, however, had other plans! I remember being very annoyed whenever they came to check the drip, or give me the next of many injections, or just to check that I was generally OK.

It seemed that between visits from the staff, my spirit seemed to leave my body, only to return when someone spoke or touched me, causing me to feel very agitated. I also felt completely frustrated as I found that I was unable to communicate with the staff. The problem was that although I could hear what they were saying to me, or about me, I couldn't answer back. Fortunately they understood the situation, and they said, 'We know you can't answer us, but we will tell you what we are doing.' They would talk to me and then go away. This continued for the whole day. The 'peace' that followed was, I am sure, 'the peace that passeth all understanding' mentioned in the Bible in Philippians 4:7. I felt wonderful, and then, after drifting into sleep, my spirit left my body and started floating down a brightly lit tunnel. It was such a wonderful feeling of happiness, joy and peace all mingled together. It seemed as though I had been travelling for ages, when suddenly the light started to get brighter and larger. Then just as I reached the end, a figure appeared and came towards me. It was Jesus. It's difficult to describe how I felt at that moment. I went out to touch Him, but He opened His arms to stop me. He had a lovely face, a big smile and very clear blue eyes that shone with such love and care – I think this picture of Him will stay with me forever. He was dressed in a robe of His time. I just stared at Him and then He said, 'Not this time, Ann, I have more work for you to do – you must go back.' At this point, my husband and my father (who died in the 1980s) came towards me. They were easily recognizable, and they guided me through the tunnel, our cloaks billowing behind us. Theirs were grey, mine was white.

As I came out of the tunnel I rested over the top of the door, and looked down over my body. I shot back into my body, through my head. My body bounced up as though I had been given an electric shock. On waking I felt fine, very peaceful and not at all disturbed.

I made a full and normal recovery following this experience. The staff were very surprised to see me looking so well the next time they entered my room. I could now communicate with them normally again. They admitted how worried they had been about me, saying that they thought they had lost me at one point. The cleaner summed up the whole situation when she came to clean my room the next day. I spotted her as she popped her head round the door. 'Come in,' I said in welcome. She stood in the doorway, looking shocked, and said, 'I expected to see you laid out – you were dying yesterday!' My next visitor was my surgeon. He too was amazed at my recovery. 'You were not well yesterday,' he admitted. 'I don't know whether to laugh or cry at the relief I feel that you're back with us – I'm delighted.'

After I had left hospital and had been recovering at home, I went for my follow-up visit. The surgeon asked if I could remember what had happened to me after my operation. I told him that I did remember and explained it all to him. He believed me and said that there was definitely something very strange happening to me. There are some, of course, who believe that it could have been the effects of the anaesthetic, but it is my belief as a Christian that what happened was real. It has made my faith even stronger. This has helped me enormously with the work that Jesus had planned for me a year later.

For nine years I have been director of the Holy Trinity Voluntary Service Scheme, caring for the elderly in the parish, including the dying and their carers. I am now retired, but continue my service, working as a chaplain. I believe God gave me this experience to enable me to sit with the dying, to help them overcome their fears and come to terms with their own death and hopefully to give them peace at the end. Through this experience I have understood that the person who dies sees no death. We pass from this world to the next in an instant, like walking from one room into another.

While I was holidaying in Israel in 1997 I had another experience of my spirit leaving my body – but it was different from the first time. Thirty-six of us from my church were visiting this ancient land, staying at a lovely hotel just outside the city walls of Jerusalem. We arrived in the early hours of Tuesday morning. The next two days were spent seeing the sights of this fascinating land, but just after sitting down for a meal in the dining room on the Wednesday evening I collapsed. I am told it was quite a while before I regained consciousness. I retired to the privacy of my hotel room, only to find that walking was now difficult. I was also in excruciating pain all over my body. The hotel staff arranged for me to see a doctor the next morning. I had a fitful night's sleep, and stayed in bed the following morning, drifting in and out of sleep, which was coupled with a wonderful sensation of peace. A passage from Psalm 139:9–10 went through my mind which said, 'If I settle on the far side of the sea, even there your hand will guide me, your right hand will hold me fast.' Then another Bible verse, this time from Deuteronomy 31:6, came to mind: 'The Lord your God goes with you, He will never leave you or forsake you', and it is this which keeps us safe in the midst of danger. Safe may not mean physical safety, but the security that holds our spirit and keeps us from despair. At this point God spoke very strongly to me. 'Listen Ann, I am talking to you. You have been working too hard. Stop and be still. Think about what I am saying, and do what I want you to do.'

At that point there was a knock on the door and the doctor came into my room. After examining me, his diagnosis was a mini-stroke, known as a transient ischaemic attack. The doctor didn't think it was necessary to be hospitalized. He suggested that I carry on with the holiday and rest as much as possible, even though that might be difficult. Four good friends looked after me. They were wonderful, because I was in fact very poorly. It had to be strength from God that enabled me to do what I did as I was so weary and tired. The coach with its cooling air conditioning helped me to stay comfortable for the many hours travelling.

On Sunday evening, we were all together in the lounge for a Holy Communion service. I collapsed yet again during the service. I was laid down on the sofa. My friends were there again, looking after me. I then once more went out of my body and floated upwards, to sit on a pure white fluffy cloud above my body. It was so peaceful, looking down on the group and watching our priest take the service. He had just blessed the bread and wine when he stopped and said, 'Let's pray for Ann.' He prayed along with all the people in the room. I felt as though I was literally being lifted and carried by prayer. I felt cocooned by warmth and love and very much in Jesus' presence. Being held in His loving arms. What an experience! At this point I returned to my body. My friends started cooling me with water, so I came to and regained consciousness as they were saying, 'She's opened her eyes, thank God she's with us again.' I understand that 15 to 20 minutes had gone by, but how peaceful I felt, and what a wonderful experience.

That peace has continued. I feel no fear of dying, a feeling accompanied by a belief that people are more important than wealth and possessions. Jesus said, 'I am the way, the truth and the life, no one comes to the Father except through me' (John 14:6). To know that we have Jesus in our lives is the most precious thing that we can have.

24 RICKY RANDOLPH

What started out as a fun hunting trip ended up as a nightmare when Ricky Randolph, a Georgia Department of Corrections officer, fell down a mountainside, badly injuring himself. But the accident brought him before his Maker, changing his attitude to life and death completely.

I was looking forward to this morning, as I had planned a hunting trip on the 98-acre farm, bordering the Chattahoochee River, where my family and I lived. I arrived home and gathered my gear, trying to get as early a start as I could. My wife had already left for work as most people do who have normal working hours. I usually called her when I was going hunting, but being in a hurry on this particular morning I didn't.

I had about a two-mile hike to my tree stand and arrived there around 10.15 a.m. My stand was about 20 feet high on the front side, facing a thick patch of pines. The back side faced the river below and dropped off to huge boulders in the river. I tied up my rifle to be pulled up after my climb to the top and began my upward ascent. I reached the top and positioned myself to pull my rifle up. Then without warning I heard a snap! I would later return to this site many times to reflect on my life. On one visit with a friend I measured the distance from the top of the stand down to the boulder I landed on – 80 feet!

As I began my fall I could see the river coming up fast. I knew this was the end for me and, though it was just seconds before impact, it was as if I was in slow motion. So many thoughts raced through my mind. My wife, my daughter, my family, and no one knows where I am! Would I ever be found? Then, darkness. How long this darkness lasted I don't know.

Then something wonderful happened. I felt myself leaving my body. I was floating a few feet in the air above the river. I looked on my body with mixed feelings. I was bleeding from my mouth, nose and ears, and saw a trickle of blood underneath me on the boulder. As I was reflecting on the state of my body, I felt a pulling and began to rise very fast. I was travelling rapidly upwards through the atmosphere.

As I left the atmosphere, I looked back and could see the Earth. Such a beautiful sight! It was so brilliantly lit. As I looked ahead I could see the planets. I thought to myself, this cannot be! Where is Jesus? I was never told anything like this could or would happen when I died! Faster and faster, the speed was increasing. I saw other star systems and galaxies as I raced onward. I entered what seemed to be a hole of some sort. It was long and dark. However, around me I saw streaks of light made up of every colour in the spectrum. I saw a faint light growing brighter and brighter in the distance up ahead. As I entered the light I felt it all through my being. I was not afraid any more.

Then, all of a sudden, I was standing before a massive set of steps. They led up to what seemed to be a bridge or walk of some kind. In the distance I saw a sight so magnificent and astounding, a city made up of what seemed to be glass or crystal.

The lights were of many colours that radiated from it. Never have I seen such a sight. I began walking toward the city in a daze of unbelief. So many questions raced through my mind. I had to know where I was. What was happening to me? I reached the front of the city and saw a double door that looked to be about 30 feet or so in height and width. It shone as if it was polished. As I stood there wondering, the doors began to open. I took a step back and looked inside. I could see what appeared to be people walking about on the inside, much as they do in a mall here on Earth. These people, though, were dressed very differently. For one thing, they all seemed to be dressed in some sort of robes with hoods. I entered through the doors in amazement at what I was seeing. The inside was massive. It seemed to be square in shape, with a balcony all around that led down to different levels. I walked up and looked downward over the balcony. It seemed to go on forever!

As I looked up I saw many passing by me, yet no one seemed to notice me. Then as one was approaching me he suddenly stopped. He slowly raised his head and I could see his face. His hair was snow white. I wanted to speak but before I could do so he turned and pointed to a long hallway. Though we never spoke I knew I was to go down this hallway. Then, as if nothing had ever happened, he continued on. I knew I had to as well.

Something was beckoning me forward. I walked a long way down to the end of this hallway. I did not turn to the right or the left. I knew somehow that my questions were about to be answered. Again I saw before me a massive double door. It seemed to be of some type of metal – whether gold or not I could not tell.

Suddenly the doors opened. I heard a voice, though not as we speak, but from inside of me it seemed, saying 'Enter!' I did as I was told and the doors shut suddenly behind me. I was afraid for the first time. Total darkness! Total silence!

Then after a space of time, the length of which I could not determine, a bright light began to glow in the room. Brighter and brighter it became. It was somewhat above me and in front of me. I tried to look but was almost blinded from it. I held my hands up in front of me and could make out the appearance of a figure sitting on some type of seat.

Without warning it happened. 'What have you done with your life?' The voice penetrated my very being. I had no answer.

Then to my right I saw what seemed to be like a movie, and I was in it! I saw my mother giving me birth, my childhood and friends. I saw everything from my youth up. I saw everything I had ever done before my very eyes.

As my life was played out before me I tried to think of good things I had done. I was raised in church and had been very active in church functions, yet as I pondered on this, I saw a man in his car that had run out of gas. I had stopped and given him a lift to a local store about a year ago. I had bought him some gas as he had no money and helped him get on his way. I thought to myself, why am I seeing this? The voice was loud and clear.

'You took no thought to help this soul and asked nothing in return. These actions are the essence of good.'

I saw all the people I had hurt as well, and was shown how my actions had set in motion the actions of others. I was stunned! I had never thought of my life having an effect on the actions that friends, family, and others I had met would take. I saw the results of all I had done. I was not pleased at all.

I looked on until the events came to an end. Indeed I had done so little with my life. I had been selfish and cruel in so many ways. I was truly sorry I had done so little. Then again, loud and clear, I heard the voice speak: 'You must return!'

I did not want to return, though. I was content to stay. I longed to stay, even after the things I had seen and heard. 'I have so many questions,' I replied. 'Things I need to know and don't understand.'

'You must return and help others to change by changing your life. Physicians will want to perform surgery on you. Do not let this happen! If you do you will never walk again. You will be visited by one who will bring you answers to the questions you have. When I call you will come again. You will recover from all that has happened if you do these things. Look and see what lies ahead.'

I turned and saw the Earth in turmoil. Wars and death, terrible sights! Cities fell and new ones were built. I saw the United States, and a volcano exploding, covering many cities in darkness. I looked on and saw the collapse of our government as we know it. People killing for food and water, horrible sights. I saw what seemed to be a giant explosion in the Earth's atmosphere and much land was destroyed.

I looked on and saw a new type of people, younger and of a peaceful nature. The cities that were left were few, but these people seemed to be content.

'It is time for you to go,' I heard again. But I wanted to see more.

The doors opened and I felt myself almost carried down the hallway. I passed out of the doors of the city and felt myself shooting into the hole through which I had come. Faster I went, unable to stop. I entered the atmosphere of Earth and saw the river below. I saw my body still lying there, motionless.

Then it was like an electric shock so tremendous I felt my body jump. I opened my eyes and saw the trees above and the skyline. Then, Oh God, the pain! I was struggling for every breath, choking on my own blood.

I managed to roll on to my stomach. The pain was all I could bear. I looked at the sky and saw the sun was lower than I remembered. I looked at my watch. It was 5.30! My only thoughts were of how could I get help. I noticed my rifle was not far from me, still attached to the rope I had tied around my waist. I began pulling it toward me. I managed to grab hold of the barrel and pulled it up to me. I fired a shot about every 10 minutes, hoping someone would come.

It was getting late and I knew I would not make it much longer, so I began crawling on my stomach, pulling myself with the stock of my rifle. I managed to crawl up a trail that ran down to the river. As I crawled and crawled, the pain was so great I passed out many times. Through thick brush and briar patches I crawled. I wanted to give up, I was so tired and in so much pain. I knew, though, I had to make it at least to where I could be found – I hoped.

I looked out in front of me and saw the road I lived on through the trees. I could hear sounds in the distance. 'Yes, thank you God,' I thought to myself.

I finally found myself at the road and began a feeble cry for help. I was too exhausted, though, and just lay in the road.

My father-in-law was returning from work and found me lying there. 'It's all right,' I heard him say, 'help is on the way.'

That was the last I remembered until I saw the lights inside the emergency room. A doctor stood at my feet.

'Can you feel this?' he said.

'Feel what?' I asked. He had been touching my feet and legs with a wooden stick. I was paralysed.

He said, 'We are sending you by ambulance to a hospital that can handle your injuries.'

Whether from the pain or medication, I was out like a light.

The next afternoon I awoke to find two doctors standing at the foot of my hospital bed. They introduced themselves as my attending physicians and proceeded to explain to me that I must undergo surgery at once. Bones in my back were broken, and were putting pressure on my spinal nerve, causing paralysis. Then I heard the warning I had heard before. 'Do not let them perform surgery, or you will never walk again!'

I understood completely, but I knew they would not. I told them I must see my wife and daughter first.

My wife arrived with my daughter shortly after the doctors' visit. I told her what they had said. She advised me that I must realize they were doing what was necessary to help me. I did not know how to tell her what I had experienced. I tried to explain it was my belief that I should not be operated on. Although she disagreed, she honoured my wishes.

When the doctors returned and I told them of my decision, they were very concerned. I listened to lecture after lecture.

That night I lay upon my bed and wept sorely. Was I insane? What was I doing?

A light began to fill my room. 'You will be well,' I heard a voice say. Then it was gone. I composed myself and dozed off to sleep.

Days turned into weeks, weeks into months. Then one morning I felt a tingling in my feet. I was overcome with joy. I told the nurse I wanted to get up and walk. I knew I was healed without a doubt.

A few hours later I was taken to the physical therapy room. They carried me down and raised me up to a vertical position. The nurse helped me in front of a set of parallel bars. I gripped the bars and placed my feet firmly on the floor. One step! Two steps.

'My God, he's walking!' the nurse said to the other who had brought me down.

The next few days were hard. I took many trips to physical therapy, and had numerous X-rays done according to my doctors' orders. My wife and family were all amazed, yet I knew. I had been told. The rest had to be true as well

My doctor was more amazed when he found there were no bones pressing on my spinal nerve. I use his quote: 'This is not normal. It seems a higher power has done for you what we were going to try and correct with surgery! I have never seen anything like this before!'

Since that day, my life has changed and I have been able to help others in ways I never dreamed. I wanted to share this with all, as it is what has led me onward in my quest for Truth.

This story may be found on the Internet at the following address:

www.webmaster@near-death.com/randolph.html

25 LOLA

Lola grew up in New York City and had a strongly Catholic background. In the summer of 1967 she had an experience that has affected her whole life ever since.

I was Catholic and was attending an all girls' parochial school. I had just turned 15 years of age and, even though growing up in the mean inner city was difficult, I loved our very diverse ethnic neighbourhood. The Irish, Greek and Jewish people who lived there had arrived from the Old World not so long before. We had Catholics and we had Jews. I really can't remember there being any Protestants and as far as I was concerned they didn't even exist.

While on vacation that summer I visited a place of such incredible natural beauty it took my breath away. As I stood there awestruck, surrounded by all this beauty, I remember thinking that if there is a God out there and He created all of this, then He must be worthy of absolute veneration and all the love we are capable of giving to Him. We returned to New York and to life as usual. I remember I had been doing some chores that day and sat down to get a little breather. My life was never to be the same again.

I felt my spirit (or what I know now was my spirit, because I never believed all that religious stuff) leave my body through the top of my head. I felt very comfortable and very natural. All of a sudden I was travelling at such an incredible velocity through the galaxies that it created an illusion of being in a tunnel. Finally I reached this place where I stopped and entered the light. My heart was melting into an ocean of unconditional and absolute love. When they say that God is love they mean this love. A love which is so utterly tender, merciful and forgiving that it is just impossible to describe in human words. I felt so wonderful, I knew I was finally home and that I had entered God's rest. Although most people don't know it, while we are on Earth we are constantly working or struggling with something. It is only after you enter His rest that you realize how much toil is involved in just living, even when we sleep.

I was in an eternal realm where past, present and future seemed all of a sudden somehow to be one and the same. The first thing I actually saw was a man in a white robe with his back to me. He was standing in front of something that seemed to be an altar. I could clearly see that the stones had been placed one on top of the other and that no tools had been used to build it. The man had a gold band around his waist and I could even see what seemed to be little bells dangling from his hem. He was sacrificing something on the altar and as he did so I could see a cloud of smoke going up. Immediately after this I was in a place where I could see the entire planet. As I was looking down at the Earth I saw a cross that was slowly being lifted up higher and higher, until it stood way up above the whole Earth. From this cross came a cloud that went around the whole circumference of the Earth. Immediately I understood that in the eyes of God this day was the most important day that ever was or that ever will be.

I was then allowed to feel the love that existed between God and Abraham. It was very real and very human. Abraham had been a friend of God. They were actually friends, can you believe it! I remember thinking how incredible this was. That is why the descendants of Abraham are very special to God, because they are the descendants of His very best friend in the whole world. It's as simple as that! I saw God weaving history with the Jewish people. He used them to bless the world and every nation where they had been scattered. His light came through them to bless all people whether they knew it or not. That is why Satan has tried from the beginning of time to destroy the Jewish people – because he is trying to hurt the work of God on this earth. The salvation of all mankind can only come through the Jewish people. Whether the Jewish people know this or not He still uses them to bless all people.

I was then shown that I myself was Jewish (something unknown to me at the time and which really didn't mean a thing to me; the Jewish people in my neighbourhood seemed nice enough but I could not understand why they never accepted Jesus). This completely blew me away – I didn't want to be Jewish any more than I wanted to be Chinese or Indian or whatever. I was shown my ancestors going from country to country with their backs hunched over, they looked so miserable. But He let me feel the tender love He felt for them through all of that. I must stop here and say this; the God of Israel, the God who created all of the Heavens and all of the Earth has not by any means forgotten His people.

Then I saw something incredible that I will never forget. It was an image of God (I can't say that I saw His face but I knew that it was God, the Father). I saw Him beckoning me to the land of Israel and letting me understand that from now on He would fight for His people. It still holds true today because God does not change; He will bless those that bless them and curse those that curse them (Genesis 12:3).

I understood the Trinity and it was just as Saint Patrick had said it was. It was like a three-leafed clover. All three were one and the one was three and all three divine. I saw a Bible open on top of a table and I understood that if I ever needed to know anything I was to go only there. I should never veer to the left or to the right, everything was contained in that Book. All this information was being given to me telepathically and I can't say that I remember hearing a single word.

I saw a large, very ornate book with names written in it, and I knew it was the Book of Life. If our name is not in that Book we will not enter the Kingdom of God. In order to enter the Kingdom of God we have to be perfect, as He is perfect. Not only do we have to be sinless but we also have to be perfect. That is why the high priests of ancient Israel had to sacrifice animals that were absolutely perfect and without even one blemish – otherwise God would not accept them as atonement for the sins of Israel.

This is where the Messiah, Jesus, comes in. He is the Lamb of God who takes away the sins of the whole world. In His infinite mercy God has provided for us a Saviour, a Redeemer, an intermediary, a high priest, a middleman and, yes, a scapegoat. On Him fell the chastisement of us all, Jew and Gentile. All the brunt of God's anger at sin and failure fell on Jesus instead of us. That is why the Jewish concept of the necessity of an Atonement for the forgiveness of sins is so important, it is the only way that we can truly understand why He had to hang on that cross for us. You see, the God of Israel cannot accept you if you are guilty of only one sin during your entire life, because the God of Israel has to see you perfect as He is perfect. Otherwise He cannot or will not accept you. Just as it is written in Leviticus, only blood can make atonement for the sins of man. Nothing else can, not good deeds or good thoughts or self-righteousness, only blood. And what exactly are we being saved from? We will go to that.

During the times of testing many people will fall away from following the God of Israel. My Bible says that all nations that forget God shall be turned into Hell. I was then taken to a place where I could see the Last Throne Judgement and then it was that I saw just what it is that we all need to be saved from. I saw the Lamb of God in all His glory. His eyes went right through the very core of my being. I threw myself at His feet and all I wanted to do was spend all eternity at His feet. They were so utterly beautiful and full of wonder, if only I could stay there forever.

I saw the Bride going through Him and emerging with beautiful white garments on. They were all going towards the likeness of someone on a throne. The joy and wonder of this scene is inexpressible. But I remember looking down and seeing people writhing in pain and screaming what seemed to me to be words of regret. They could actually look up and see these people going into an eternity full of joy and they themselves could have been among them. They could have been saved from their horrible fate of eternity in Hell. I heard their cries and saw the anguish on their faces, and my heart broke for them.

The God of Israel does not want even one soul to go there. I pray every day that not even my worst enemy will go there. The persons that have hurt me the most, oh God, I pray, please don't let them go there. Oh God, please let me keep just one person from going there. Even if I do nothing else in my whole life I will be happy with just that gift, even if that person is my worst enemy! Remember the story of Lazarus? How Jesus told us that the rich man was begging to have Lazarus go to his family to warn them of this place of torment lest they also go there? The answer to him was that if they hadn't believed Moses and the prophets, why would they believe a person though he rises from the dead to warn them? The rich man ended up in Hell not because he was a bad man – because it doesn't say that he was – but he was rich and had received all his good things while on the Earth, and poor Lazarus had only received bad things.

When Jesus told us this story He was not giving us a parable, He was stating a fact. People of God, wake up! If we are rich only towards the things of this world and not rich towards God, what will we be when all those things are taken away from us? Will we be able to stand on the last day? Let us all repent, myself included, from worthless acts centred only around the here and now and let us ground and centre ourselves around the God of Israel and his Holy Word. Then and only then will we be counted worthy of the atonement He has provided for us!

My Bible says that all of Israel will be saved, and I believe that to be true. How He will do that, I certainly do not know, but I do know that with God all things are possible. God loves the most worthless sinner. If we truly love God as we say we do, then we must love that worthless sinner and hate the sin. We must be like Moses and plead with God Himself for the salvation of His people. God curse me but save them! Our love should be that strong and that real! God does not see the colour of our skins; He does not care how much money we have or how many diplomas we have earned. God does not see our denominations because our denominations will not save us, the Blood of the Lamb will. One thing and one thing only will be asked of us when we get to that other side: How much did you love, my child?

This story may be found on the Internet at the following address:

www.pconline.com/~jsenear/LOLA.HTM

26 SIMON MACKRELL

The roads of New Zealand are not known for their congestion, and in the main are reasonably free of traffic. But accidents can happen even on country roads, as Simon Mackrell found one rainy morning in October 1990. The accident he was involved in took him both to Heaven – and Hell.

I had worked as a fitter and welder in a maintenance workshop since December 1988. On 19 October 1990 I was travelling to Kawerau in a utility truck, towing a 16-foot tandem trailer carrying a four-cylinder diesel motor. It was a heavy load.

When I left Mount Maunganui at 7.30 a.m. the weather was rainy. At about 8.20 a.m., when approaching the single-lane underpass at Matata, the utility hit the trailer of a truck-and-trailer unit. On the approach, I had been touching the brakes to slow down without skidding, since the road had become slippery and wet. Whether I hit the brakes too hard the final time or the discs had heated up I'm not sure, but the utility skidded and hit the wheels of the trailer of the truck.

I knew that any truck units coming through the underpass needed to make use of the whole road to get through and that was why I was travelling slowly and carefully. When I saw the trailer of the truck unit tracking down my side of the road, I got as far to the left as possible but skidded down the opposite camber of the road into the wheels of the trailer. The impact pushed the utility backwards and spun it around slightly. The trailer wheel's hub shoved in the bonnet of the utility and broke the mixer off the carburettor. The utility was a dual-fuel vehicle, using either liquid petroleum gas or petrol. That day it was running on liquid petroleum gas and immediately burst into flames. The weight of the utility trailer and the impact caused the bolts of the utility towbar to shear, the trailer drawbar hit the tank and dropped the liquid petroleum gas cylinder on to the road. At impact, the gas ignited and the flames engulfed the vehicle. The flames poured in at the driver's door.

All the above happened so quickly that I panicked, and my life seemed to flash before my eyes. I fought to free myself and could hear strange voices. Yet somehow I was comforted by the Holy Spirit saying, 'Be calm, my hand is on you, undo the seat belt, open the door, My protection is with you and I will help you.' As He was speaking I did what He was saying. I thought the door may have jammed in the frame, so I lifted the handle and rammed my shoulder against the door. The door burst open and I flew out sideways towards the road, yet I landed on my feet. I felt a hand on my collar pulling me to my feet. I presumed that this was the hand of the truck driver who had stopped to help me, but he said that the flames had been too hot, and that he had only helped me to my feet after I had rolled in the wet grass and a puddle to extinguish my burning overalls. When he touched me he got a fright as some of my skin stuck to his hand. He told me later that he had not expected to see me come out of the vehicle alive.

He helped me to move up the road away from the burning utility which was exploding in the heat of the flames. He sat me on a raincoat on the embankment between the road and the railway line, and doused my burns with water. I felt hot and dry inside, so I indicated the need for a drink. Following the first gulp of water, I wanted to scream in pain, but when I opened my mouth only a 'Sh, sh' sound came out. This was the first indication that my injuries were serious, and that I had internal burning. I was to learn later that not only had I between 35 and 40 per cent external burns, but I was also burnt from my mouth to my stomach and had burnt both lungs. The driver had trouble contacting the emergency services because the site where the accident happened is a radio dead spot. He fortunately managed to make contact with an approaching truck, and he was able to relay the message for help. There was an ambulance already on a journey to Edgecumbe, so it didn't have to start from its base; in the end it came to my aid much quicker than the other services.

On the way to hospital I was thanking the Lord for everything He had done for me. As I started thanking Him, the pain and shock increased. I would have passed out, but I asked the Lord for help, as I wished to continue to praise Him for His goodness in rescuing me. The pain did not go away completely but it remained at a level I could tolerate, which was in line with 1 Corinthians 10:13b which says: 'I will not test you beyond that which you can handle and with every testing, I will provide a means of escape.' I believe my escape was in prayer, praise and praying in tongues.

I remained conscious when they wheeled me into accident and emergency at the local hospital. I was even able to chat and joke with the staff while they cut off the remains of my burnt overalls and clothing. The anaesthetist then put me into a deep coma so that they could prepare me for the skin grafting I would need.

Burns patients are put into an induced coma and placed on life support machines to sustain and monitor vital signs so that any loss of body fluids may be treated. I was given morphine to prepare me for the helicopter flight to another large hospital, which has the most modern and well-equipped burns treatment facilities. I was treated with morphine, blood and plasma.

I have two memories of this period. The first memory was on Thursday of the first week. I woke from the anaesthetic some time after one of the many operations that I was to endure. My body was aching all over and I was shaking terribly. I tried to talk to the black African male nurse looking after me, but was unable to because of a tube in my mouth. The second memory was from some time during the middle weekend when my lungs played up, collapsing one after the other, and my heart experienced disturbances of rhythm. The medical team worked around the clock for about two days to keep me alive. At one point during this time my spirit seemed to leave my body, giving me what is known as a near-death experience.

It was like being in a deep sleep, in a favourite chair, and then being woken suddenly, and thinking that you have been asleep longer than you really have. Instead of waking and seeing normal sunlight, or white electrical light, I was in a place which appeared to be lit with poor infra-red lights, as if I had stepped into a photographer's darkroom. When I was aware of the light I experienced a chilling fear, a blood-curdling cold, and I was descending into a chasm. As I descended deeper the chasm got darker, and I experienced waves of oppression, anguish, pain, agony and loneliness. It was like being tortured from within and from outside my being. The fear and cold penetrated right through me. I put my hands to my head to comfort myself and my hands passed right through my body. I was in the spirit, having shape but no form. It was then that I heard screams, cries and wailings coming from where I was heading. The smell was also terrible. At this moment I felt myself saying, 'I'm going the wrong way, I should be going up, this is Hell. I'm of the Lord Jesus Christ. Lord save me, please. You're the resurrection and the life.' When I mentioned Jesus the place erupted with foul language and voices telling me in no uncertain terms to shut up.

I had only got out the words 'I'm of the Lord Jesus Christ' when a bright light surrounded me from head to toe. The light dispelled the darkness and it was full of love, peace, joy and a real feeling of security. In the light I smelt an amazing fragrance. The light came down from above, while below it, and running parallel to it, was a path of golden stones or cobblestones. I was lifted by what seemed like two hands, one on each of my hips, and I was drawn up the light along the path. Soon it levelled out. Before me were the walls of a huge city. They reminded me of the walls I had seen in the film *Jesus of Nazareth*, but instead of the walls being a brown or tan colour as in the film, these walls were multicoloured and shimmering from the light. The colours were in layers, reflecting the gems they were made from. The Bible describes the gems of the walls in Revelation 21. The beauty was amazing and glorious, more beautiful than a rainbow or anything on Earth.

The path ended at the huge white gate which the Bible calls the gates of pearl. The same light in which I was moving radiated out from within the city, containing the same love, peace, joy and warmth. As I stood at the gates, I heard amazing singing coming from within the city, voices that sang in beautiful harmony and melody, singing to the Lord.

I'm not sure if the angel stepped through the gate or if he was there all the time, but only when he spoke to me did I become aware of his presence. He said, 'Return to where you came from.' I put my arms out, pointing into the city, and said, 'I'm home, I'd like to go to be with my Lord Jesus and with my Abba Daddy.' He replied, 'The Lord's return is imminent, I have more to do, you are to return to where you came from.' The angel was huge, above seven or eight feet tall. He was broad, dressed in a white robe with sandals on his feet. He had a leather belt around him that held a big sword in an ornamented sheath. The belt was braided with gold and brass thread. He had an amazing presence and spoke with the authority of God.

Just as I had been drawn up the path in the light, now I moved away from the city, and it was all darkness again. I still had my arms outstretched, so when my spirit returned to my body my arms lifted up. When my mum came in one day, the nurse commented that my arms had been raised. They had wondered if I had been praying or hallucinating, although they weren't sure. But something had happened and they comforted Mum by saying I had turned a corner and was much better. Mum wishes she had noted the time and date in her notebook because from that moment on until I came out of the coma, my healing accelerated rapidly.

A fortnight after the accident, on a Friday afternoon, I woke from the coma. The doctors withdrew my respiratory tube, since they assessed that I was breathing well enough on my own. I had two gastric tubes in me and was still attached to the life support monitor. But then on Saturday morning, not long after morning tea, and while trying to attract the attention of the nurse, I ripped out a tube from the carotid artery, which is a major artery in the blood supply between the heart and the brain. If the tube is not withdrawn carefully it can damage the artery, or if the wound is not sealed with pressure a lot of blood is lost. The nurse rushed in and applied pressure to my neck at the position of the artery but was amazed to find no blood flowing from the wound, nor any internal bleeding. Later in the day the doctors took me off the life support monitor and left only a drip in my arm to supply a food solution and fluid.

I was discharged from hospital on 1 January 1991, having made steady progress, and having been able to talk and pray with several patients about my faith in God.

What happened to me was real, and the things that I have seen and experienced are not of my making or my own doing. They are what God did, directly or through others in answer to their prayers of faith. The love and support both Mum and I received from our immediate family and friends were tremendous. So was the support we received from our church and the pastoral team. I am also thankful for the encouragement and letters from Christians I received while in hospital.

As Christians, I believe that we should not be spiritual secret agents, but also be willing to share our good news with others.

27 HOW DO WE KNOW THAT GOD EXISTS?

In order to be sure about these near-death stories we need to know more about the God behind the experiences, and whether we can indeed believe that He is real.

The authors gratefully acknowledge Chuck Missler's research in his excellent audiocassette briefing package, *The Creator Beyond Time and Space*. The authors would also like to thank Chuck Missler for his kind permission to quote this research in this book. Chuck Missler's ministry address and web site details are given at the end of this book under 'Further Information'.

This material is also available in the excellent book, *The Creator Beyond Time and Space* by Mark Eastman MD and Chuck Missler (The Word For Today Publishers, 1996). This recommended book is also available from Chuck Missler's ministry or web site.

In Genesis 1:1 the Bible states, 'In the beginning God created the heavens and the earth'. Until the early part of the 20th century the Western world held this predominantly Judeo-Christian world view. There has been a dramatic shift from this view, mainly due to the increasing acceptance of the theory of evolution, following the publication in 1859 of *The Origin of Species* by Charles Darwin. The theory of evolution developed into the atheistic 'Spontaneous Generation' theory, which stated that all life on planet Earth descended from a common single cell, arising by chance in the primordial ooze, 3.5 billion years ago.

Over the last 100 years there has been a dramatic shift from the Biblical Creation model to the Spontaneous Generation model, which is now widely taught in schools and universities. The fact is that the Spontaneous Generation model does not stand up to close inspection, as many modern scientists have now agreed.

The universe had a finite beginning

Albert Einstein published his Special Theory of Relativity in 1905, and his General Theory of Relativity in 1915. In 1968 and 1970 three British astrophysicists, Steven Hawking, George Ellis and Roger Penrose, published papers in which they extended Einstein's Theory of General Relativity to include measurements of time and space. According to their papers, time and space had a finite beginning that corresponded to the origin of matter and energy. Prior to this moment, time and space did not exist! (Steven Hawking and George Ellis, 'The Cosmic Black-body Radiation and the Existence of Singularities of our Universes', *Astrophysical Journal*, 152 (1968), pp.25–36; Steven Hawking and Roger Penrose, 'The Singularities of Gravitational Collapse and Cosmology', *Proceedings of the Royal Society of London*, Series A, 314 (1970), pp. 529–548.)

The Spontaneous Generation theory contradicts the most basic laws of physics

To explain the origin of matter in the atheistic Spontaneous Generation model, it is simply assumed that matter arose from nothing. This is in direct contravention of the First Law of Thermodynamics, according to which matter cannot create itself. (The First Law of Thermodynamics states that the sum of kinetic energy, potential energy and thermal energy in a closed system remains constant. In other words, matter, or its energy equivalent, cannot be created or destroyed under natural circumstances. This law is often thought of as the Law of Conservation of Mass and Energy.) There must therefore have been an 'outside agency'. The Bible describes this as God, who created everything.

In Darwin's Theory of Evolution, and the Spontaneous Generation model, it is proposed that 'simple life' evolved into more complex life forms. Darwin's Theory of Evolution and the Spontaneous Generation model both directly contravene the Second Law of Thermodynamics, which states that disorder in a system increases, rather than decreases. The Second Law of Thermodynamics implies that the universe could not order and provide energy for itself. (The Second Law of Thermodynamics gives a precise definition of a property called entropy. Entropy can be thought of as a measure of the disorder in a system. The law states that the entropy, or disorder, of an isolated system can never decrease. In other words, in our universe, a state of order progresses to a state of disorder.) The order and energy observed in the universe again implies an 'outside agency', whom the Bible describes as God.

Comments from world-famous scientists

The words of many prominent scientists cast doubt upon the kind of universe proposed by the Spontaneous Generation theory. In 1930 British physicist Sir James Jeans wrote:

Nature seems very conversant with the rules of pure mathematics ... In the same way, a scientific study of the action of the universe has suggested a conclusion which may be summed up ... in the statement that the universe appears to have been designed by a pure mathematician ... the universe can best be pictured, although still very imperfectly and inadequately, as consisting of pure thought ... If the universe is a universe of thought, then its creation must have been an act of thought. Indeed the finiteness of space compels us to think of the creator as working outside time and space, which are part of his creation, just as an artist is outside his canvas. (*The Mysterious Universe*, Macmillan, 1930, p. 146)

NASA astronomer Robert Jastrow wrote some years later:

Now we see how the astronomical evidence leads to a Biblical view of the origin of the world: the chain of events leading to man commenced suddenly and sharply in a definite moment of time, in a flash of light and energy. (*God and the Astronomers*, Norton, 1992, p. 14)

Sir Fred Hoyle has spent many years studying the origins of life. He has commented:

A super-intellect has monkeyed with physics, as well as with chemistry and biology. ('The Universe, Past and Present Reflection', *Annual Reviews of Astronomy and Astrophysics*, 20:16, 1982)

The likelihood of the formation of life from inanimate matter is one to a number with 40 thousand noughts (zeros) after it. It is enough to bury Darwin and the whole Theory of Evolution. There was no primeval soup, neither on this planet nor on any other, and if the beginnings of life were not random they must therefore have been the product of a purposeful intelligence. (*Nature*, vol. 294:105, 12 Nov. 1981)

The astronomer George Greenstein has recently given his thoughts:

As we survey all the evidence, the thought instantly arises that some supernatural agency – or rather Agency – must be involved. Is it possible that suddenly, without intending to, we have stumbled upon the existence of a Supreme Being? Was it God who stepped in and so providentially crafted the cosmos for our benefit? (*The Symbiotic Universe*, New York: William Morrow, 1998, p. 27)

Physicist and Nobel laureate Arno Penzias, too, insists on the necessity for a Creator:

Astronomy leads us to a unique event, an universe which was created out of nothing, one with a very delicate balance needed to provide exactly the conditions required to permit life, and one which has an underlying (one might say 'supernatural') plan. (Henry Margenau and Roy Varghese, eds., *Cosmos, Bios, and Theos*, La Salle, IL: Open Court, 1992, p. 83)

Robert Shapiro comments on the likelihood of life arising out of nothing:

The improbability involved in generating even one bacterium is so large that it reduces all considerations of time and space to nothingness. Given such odds, the time until the black holes evaporate and the space to the ends of the universe would make no difference at all. If we were to wait, we would truly be waiting for a miracle. (*Origins – A Skeptic's Guide to the Creation of Life on Earth*, p. 105)

In 1982 Francis Crick, winner of the Nobel Prize for biology, noted:

An honest man, armed with all the knowledge available to us now, could only state that in some sense, the origin of life appears at the moment to be almost a miracle, so many are the conditions which would have to be satisfied to get it going. (*Life Itself, Its Origin and Nature*, London: Futura, 1982)

In summary, there are such difficulties reconciling the Spontaneous Generation theory of the evolution of life with observable laws of physics that modern and respected scientists have seriously questioned the whole theory.

The Biblical view of the universe, created by God Himself, is the only, and the correct, alternative. It is also by far the simplest!

The real you is software, not hardware!

The following figures are taken from Chuck Missler's excellent briefing package, *The ET Scenario*. The real you was chosen before the foundation of the world, and has no time dimension. In other words the real you is immortal.

Each human body contains approximately 75 trillion cells. Each cell, except for the red blood cells, has a full complement of chromosomes in its nucleus. Each nucleus has 46 chromosomes made up of 23 pairs, one from each of the two parents of each individual. Each chromosome contains a strand of DNA, which includes hundreds of millions of base pairs. Stretched out straight, each strand of DNA would measure 3–9 feet long and about 20 atoms across.

DNA was discovered in 1952. DNA is composed of adenine, thymidine, guanine and cytosine. DNA is the computer storage medium of the human body. DNA is in fact a three-out-of-four digital code, with immense storage capacity. Each particular cell in the human body has a particular computer code, with information about how it should function, repair itself and reproduce. DNA is an extremely complex molecule.

It can be calculated mathematically, using Switching Theory, that the chance of one DNA molecule occurring randomly is one chance in 10^{57} (Chuck Missler: *The ET Scenario*). The scientific community discounts any 'chance' greater than one chance in 10^{50}, which means that DNA could not possibly have evolved by Spontaneous Generation. This invalidates completely the notion of Man being formed from 'primitive cells'. The fact is that 'primitive cells' are not primitive. They have DNA in them, which is incredibly complex, and simply could not have 'evolved by chance'.

In the animal kingdom, the human, the rat, the bat, the mouse, the worm and the fruit fly all have the same DNA code. If we were to discover different computers using identical software we could safely assume that all the computers obtained their software from the same software house. Thus all DNA codes of life came from the same 'software house', proving the supernatural origin of life on this planet. Each individual is thus pre-programmed, and that program resides on the DNA in each individual cell comprising our human body. The DNA code includes details of our height, our personality, our intelligence, the colours of our eyes and other physical attributes. It is for this reason that family likeness is readily observed.

Just as software may be loaded on to a floppy diskette, so our software is loaded on to our DNA. In the analogy of a diskette, the weight of the disk remains the same whether megabytes of information are present on the diskette or not. Real computer information in a computer is weightless software, rather than the plastic and metal of the actual hardware.

In the same way, your real personality, the real 'you', is weightless, timeless software, coded on your DNA. The real 'you' is immortal. According to Jesus Christ one day we will all be resurrected. 'For the hour is coming in which all who are in the grave will hear His voice and come forth – those who have done good, to the resurrection of life, and those who have done evil to the resurrection of damnation' (John 5:28, 29).

To further confound the sceptics Sir Fred Hoyle calculated the odds of only the proteins of an amoeba arising by chance as one chance in $10^{40,000}$ (Chuck Missler: *The Creator Beyond Time and Space*).

Difficulties with information systems

There is not space in this book to develop this theme fully. However, there are immeasurable difficulties in this area with respect to the Spontaneous Generation model, which are briefly touched on below. Assuming that DNA could 'evolve by chance', the Spontaneous Generation model still has major difficulties.

DNA is a digital information system, which sends highly complicated and specific instructions to each cell within which it resides. If the reader imagines DNA as a highly complex modern cellular phone, capable of sending digital codes to other cellular phones, then the size of the problem becomes apparent. How is it that this highly complex 'cellular phone', which 'developed spontaneously', can send digital messages to countless other 'cellular phones', on exactly the same frequency, in a computer language which other 'cellular phones' can understand and act on? The fact is that there is no information system known to man that does not require 'programming' by an outside agency. If cellular phones were able to manufacture themselves, you can guarantee that they would not be able to communicate with each other. They would only be able to communicate with each other when an outside agency, of greater technological expertise, programmed all the cellular phones to identical frequencies, using identical computer languages.

Left- and right-handed forms of molecules and proteins in living systems

The problem increases when the molecular biology of the living cell is studied. In all living systems molecules of DNA and RNA exist in the right-hand form (they are dextrorotatory). The amino acids in all living systems are in the left-hand form (they are levorotatory). Even supposing that these complex molecules and proteins were to evolve from a primordial ooze, consisting of basic elements, the product would be a racemic mixture of both left- and right-handed forms of DNA, RNA, and amino acids. This racemic mixture of left- and right-handed forms would be completely useless for living cells, completely distorting the architecture of these complex cell structures. In the cellular phone analogy, if you cross the wiring over within the phone, producing 'mirror image wiring', you can guarantee that the cellular phone will not work!

In summary

The Spontaneous Generation model is faced with such huge problems that independent-thinking individuals, understanding the problems involved, would be much better advised to accept the only plausible alternative: 'In the beginning God created the heavens and the earth' (Genesis 1:1).

28 HOW DO WE KNOW THAT THE BIBLE IS A SUPERNATURAL BOOK, INSPIRED BY GOD HIMSELF?

We have now established that God is real and involved in His creation, but how can we know what His purposes are for us? For this, we turn to the Bible, to try and discover whether it can be trusted.

Christians believe that the Bible is the supernaturally inspired Word of God mainly because Jesus Christ said that it was. There is, however, considerable other evidence about the unique origin of scripture. This section seeks to show that the scriptures, the book we call the Holy Bible, could only have been inspired by a supernatural intelligence living completely outside our human experience.

What did Jesus Christ say about the Bible?

Jesus said in his last prayer that 'Your Word is Truth' (John 17:17). Jesus himself freely quoted scripture and was obviously extremely conversant with it. He was, after all, a Jewish rabbi!

The Bible at the time of Jesus Christ was the Old Testament. It was the Old Testament which Jesus knew so well, and from which he quoted so freely. Jesus in fact put his own authority on scripture in the following statement: 'Heaven and Earth will pass away, but my words will not pass away' (Matthew 24:35).

Paul declared in the New Testament that 'All Scripture is given by inspiration of God' (2 Timothy 3:16).

Other indications of the supernatural origins of scripture

Readers of this book may not be familiar with the supernatural origin of scripture, which is taken very lightly by large sections of our society. It is hoped that the following will add considerably to the understanding of the unique, supernatural origin of scripture.

Prophecy
The Bible is a prophetic book. It clearly foretells the future because God lives outside our fourth dimension, known as Time. Jesus Christ said, 'before Abraham was born, I am' (John 8:58), confirming that He existed before the birth of Abraham. The Bible states that Jesus Christ is God, and pre-existed everything (John 1:1).

Over 25 per cent of the Bible refers to future events. The most mathematically amazing scripture is found in Daniel 9:25–26. In this scripture the angel Gabriel is foretelling the exact date when Jesus Christ, the anticipated Messiah, would come to Jerusalem. It is completely accurate to the very day. 'Know and understand that from the issuing of a decree to restore and rebuild Jerusalem until Messiah the Prince there will be seven weeks and sixty-two weeks ...then after the sixty two weeks the Messiah will be cut off ...'

A concise explanation of this is given in the *New American Standard Bible* (New Open Bible Study Edition, p. 942):

The vision of the sixty-nine weeks in Daniel 9:25, 26 pinpoints the coming of the Messiah. The decree of Daniel

9:25 took place on March 4th, 444 BC (Nehemiah 2:1–8). The sixty-nine weeks of seven years equals 483 years, or 173,880 days (using 360-day prophetic years*). This leads to March 29th, AD 33, the date of the Triumphal Entry (of Jesus into Jerusalem). This is checked by noting that 444 BC to AD 33 is 476 years, and 476 times 365.24219 days per year equals 173,855 days. Adding 25 days for the difference between March 4th and March 29th gives 173,880 days.

*It should be noted that the Babylonians used a 360-day calendar, which must be converted to our current solar years, of 365 days. These 360-day years are commonly called prophetic years.

This prophecy is mathematically correct to the precise day. There is simply no other book on Earth which predicts the future with such stunning accuracy.

The recurrent number seven found in the Bible
In the Bible the number seven is the number of God. There are myriad chains and sequences of sevens found in both the text, and the Hebrew and Greek numerics, of scripture. In this respect the Bible is unique, and clearly of supernatural design.

A more detailed analysis of the number seven in scripture is beyond the scope of this book, but our account summarizes Chuck Missler's work *Beyond Coincidence* in which he demonstrates the supernatural authority of the Bible, quoting the famous work of the Russian mathematician Ivan Panin (1855–1942).

Matthew 1:1–16 concerns the names of ancestors of Jesus Christ. The following observations may be made about this passage:

- The number of words is divisible by seven.
- The number of letters is divisible by seven.
- The number of vowels is divisible by seven.
- The number of consonants is divisible by seven.
- The number of words beginning with a vowel is divisible by seven.
- The number of words beginning with a consonant is divisible by seven.
- The number of words that occur more than once is divisible by seven.
- The number of words that occur in only one form is divisible by seven.
- The number of nouns is divisible by seven.
- Only seven words are not nouns.
- The number of names is divisible by seven.
- Only seven other kinds of noun are present.
- The number of male names is divisible by seven.
- The number of generations is divisible by seven.

The implications of the above lists of names, and characteristics associated with those names, are simply beyond the ability of man to comprehend. It would be extremely difficult for anyone to construct a list of names with these characteristics. It is quite impossible for anyone to arrange the name of his own father, let alone names of members of the family tree in many preceding generations. Only God could have arranged this, conclusively proving the supernatural authenticity of scripture.

The signature of God in the first five books of the Bible
Chuck Missler has given us permission to quote his information regarding the findings in the Hebrew text of the Torah, the first five books of the Bible (Chuck Missler, *The Cosmic Codes*).

Rabbi Michael Ber Weissmandl discovered the 'signature of God' in the first five books of the Bible. These five books, Genesis, Exodus, Leviticus, Numbers and Deuteronomy, are known by the Jewish community as the *Torah*. Readers may be more familiar with the Greek translation of *Torah,* namely the *Pentateuch.* In fact *Torah* is the English translation of the Hebrew word *Torh.*

Similarly we are familiar with the name of God, *Yahweh,* commonly described as *Jehovah.* Both of these are English transliterations of the actual Hebrew word *Yhwh.*

In the original Hebrew text of the Torah, the Hebrew equivalent letters T, O, R, H are spelled out every 50th letter at the beginning of Genesis and Exodus. That is to say, that if you take the first letter T *(tau)* in the book of Genesis and then count 49 letters the next letter will be the letter O *(vav),* and so on.

In the books of Numbers and Deuteronomy the same signature of God applies, although the letters TORH are found backwards, both pointing to the central book of Leviticus. Chuck Missler has calculated that the chance of the name TORH appearing at the beginning of the text of both Genesis and Exodus is about one in three million.

At the beginning of the book of Leviticus the name YHWH is found in the text every seventh letter, starting with the letter Y *(yod).*

The chances of the five separate constructions, all appearing only at the beginning of the five books of the Torah, must be one chance in trillions, proving again that the whole Bible is totally supernatural.

There are many other aspects of the authenticity of scripture beyond the scope of this book. It is recommended that the reader listens to *The Cosmic Codes*, Chuck Missler's excellent briefing package.

The Gates of the Heavenly City

Another interesting confirmation of scripture is identified by D.H.A. Woodward in his book *Gems from the City*. He has done a scientific study of the 28 precious and semiprecious stones known on Earth. These are gemstones with hardness measuring over seven on the Mohs' Scale.

He found that if particles of all 28 stones are examined under a microscope using plane polarized light, only 12 of the 28 stones will refract this light, producing rainbow colours as described in scripture. These are the 12 listed by John in Revelation 21:18–20.

Woodward has calculated that, on a purely mathematical basis, the chances of John picking the correct 12 gemstones, out of 28 gemstones, is one in 30 million. This is one further mathematical proof of the supernatural origin of scripture. (*Gems from the City*, The Emerald Charitable Foundation, PO Box 414, Quinton, Birmingham B17 8LQ, England, 1984.)

29 HOW DO WE KNOW THAT JESUS CHRIST IS THE MESSIAH?

Many men, before and since the birth of Jesus of Nazareth, have claimed to be the Messiah. So how can we be sure that Jesus was who He said He was – the anointed One of God? The evidence is set out for you to see in this chapter. The answer to the question 'How do we know that Jesus Christ is the Messiah?' can be answered in various ways, as follows:

Jesus said so

'The high priest asked Him, saying unto Him, "Are You the Christ, the Son of the Blessed?" Jesus said, "I am."' (Mark 14:61–62)

Prophecy

The Bible has over 300 prophecies which were fulfilled in the New Testament. The following is a sample of eight prophecies concerning the coming of the Messiah, Jesus, in the Old Testament, which were all fulfilled in the New Testament, often many hundreds of years later.

In his excellent study *Footprints of the Messiah*, Chuck Missler has examined eight of the 300 prophecies fulfilled by the Lord Jesus in His ministry while here on Earth.

The laws of probability

Before giving the details it is important to understand the laws of probability. If we imagine a room in which there are 100 people, of whom 50 per cent are men and 50 per cent are women, there is a 1:2 probability of any individual in that room, taken at random, being a man. If it is assumed that 50 per cent of the people in this particular room are left-handed, and 50 per cent are right-handed, then there is a 1:2 probability of an individual chosen at random being left-handed.

The probability of the two separate probabilities must be compounded to obtain the chance of choosing, at random, an individual in the room who is both male and left-handed. Therefore, mathematically, the chance of choosing a left-handed male in this particular room of 100 people is 1:4. In other words, using the laws of probability there is a one-in-four chance of an individual, chosen at random, being both male and left-handed.

The chances of Jesus Christ fulfilling eight prophecies

The following short study sets out to enumerate mathematically the chances of one individual at the time of the life of Jesus Christ fulfilling eight well-known Old Testament prophecies. The prophecies chosen by Chuck Missler are the following:

1 Micah 5:2 – Jesus was born in Bethlehem, fulfilled Matthew 2:1, 6.
2 Zechariah 9:9 – The Messiah came riding on a donkey, fulfilled Matthew 21:1–11.
3 Zechariah 11:12 – The Messiah was betrayed for 30 pieces of silver, fulfilled in Matthew 26:15 and 27:9.
4 Zechariah 11:13 – The money was used by the temple authorities to buy a potter's field, fulfilled Matthew 27:3–8.

5 Zechariah 13:6 – Describes the wounds in the hands of Jesus in the house of his friends, fulfilled John 20:25.
6 Isaiah 53:7 – 'He was oppressed and afflicted yet he opened not his mouth', fulfilled Matthew 27:12–14.
7 Isaiah 53:9 – 'And they made his grave with the wicked but with the rich in his death', fulfilled Matthew 27:57–60.
8 Psalm 22:16 – 'They pierced my hands and my feet', fulfilled John 20:25.

Conclusion

Using the laws of probability, Chuck Missler has calculated in the book *Footprints of the Messiah* that the probability of these eight prophecies being fulfilled by one individual is $1:10^{28}$.

Further mathematical analysis of this large number

The estimate of the number of people who have actually lived on this planet is approximately 10^{11}. The chance of one actual person in history fulfilling all eight prophecies is $1:10^{28}$ divided by 10^{11}, which equals $1:10^{17}$.

This is, however, only for eight prophecies! Doing some simple mathematics, the chance of Jesus fulfilling 16 prophecies comes to $1:10^{45}$. The chance of Jesus fulfilling just 48 prophecies is $1:10^{157}$.

Large numbers in perspective

These huge numbers need to be put into perspective. Some scientists believe that the universe is 10 billion years old. There are 10^{17} seconds in 10 billion years. In other words the chances of one second being chosen in the history of the universe is $1:10^{17}$.

For Jesus to fulfil over 300 prophecies, as He did, the laws of probability dictate that the fact that Jesus Christ is the Messiah is the single most likely event in the history of our universe, and absolutely nothing comes remotely close!

The name of God above the cross

When Jesus was crucified the following sign was placed above Him, in Hebrew, Greek and Latin. The Hebrew version read:

Yeshua HaNazarei wMelech HaYehudim

meaning 'Jesus the Nazarean and King of the Jews'. Reading the first letters of the Hebrew inscription we read Y, H, W, H. This is the name of God, above the cross of Jesus Christ, the Messiah, who is God.

30 WHY I BELIEVE IN THE RESURRECTION

by Dr John Sloan FRCS, FFAEM, Consultant in Accident & Emergency, Leeds General Infirmary, UK

People down the ages have set out to disprove the resurrection of Jesus, only to be convinced by the facts that it really did happen the way the Bible describes. In this chapter Dr John Sloan gives his reasons for believing in the resurrection of Jesus Christ.

As a Christian doctor, people often wonder how it is that I can, on the one hand, believe factual and scientific information, while, on the other, being 'religious'. It is a very reasonable area for consternation. Most are too polite to ask, of course.

Let me say at the outset that I don't think I am a very religious person, and I have little time for pomp and ceremony. My Christianity revolves around a relationship with Jesus Christ, and what I do flows from that precious relationship. As such, I find that my faith in the risen Christ, and my profession, not only co-exist but are mutually supportive. I will return to this point later. At this stage I would like to make this statement, and for a number of years I have been very clear on this one point: *it is a fact that Jesus died and rose*. And, this being so, His claims are true, and Christianity stands. But what is the basis for my faith in the resurrection? Have I needed to throw reason overboard? I would like to present three separate aspects, which indicate that there is a reason for my faith. I will summarize these, and then I will expand on each:

1 Firstly, the evidence indicating that Jesus died and rose from the dead is overwhelming.

2 Secondly, specific details surrounding the crucifixion and resurrection were foretold.

3 Thirdly, the risen Christ can be known and He can change us.

Before the reader considers the next section, it is important to note that it is graphic in medical detail, which some may find distressing.

The evidence indicating that Jesus died and rose from the dead is overwhelming

That Jesus died is beyond doubt. The medical evidence is overwhelming, quite apart from the contemporary historical accounts.

Medical evidence

Most days I deal with people who have been injured. The pattern of injuries people sustain gives a great deal of information about what caused them. In fact, I often have to attend court cases to give evidence under oath concerning people's injuries, and how likely their accounts are to be true. The pattern of injuries inflicted on Jesus gives an immense amount of information about what happened to Him.

The Roman practice of that time meant that Jesus' scourging would have been carried out with leather whips. Pieces of bone and lead were woven into the leather thongs, so that maximal injury resulted. The effect of this type of scourging would have been to create severe skin and underlying fat and muscle damage. Initial blood and fluid loss would have been considerable. After the initial loss, slow loss would have occurred in a way not dissimilar to a burn. The area damaged would equate to about

15 per cent of body surface area, and fluid loss from this would be 1–2 litres over eight hours, assuming Jesus' weight to be 70kg (the weight of an average adult male).

His scalp was bleeding from the thorns. The scalp is very rich with blood vessels, and bleeding would have been considerable, further adding to fluid loss. It is very likely that blood losses of 250–500ml occurred in this way.

Then He carried a heavy cross (the cross beam to be precise) and walked some distance in this state. The ensuing exhaustion would have resulted in profound sweat loss, further compounding his fluid depletion. So, without considering crucifixion, Jesus lost over 2 litres, most of which was blood or plasma. This low volume (hypovolaemic) state is characterized by a fall in blood pressure, a racing heart beat (tachycardia) and an elevated respiratory rate (tachypnoea).

A 70kg man would be expected to have 5 litres of circulating blood volume. Loss of up to 2 litres (30–40 per cent) is defined as class III shock. Loss of more than 2 litres (over 40 per cent) is class IV shock and is life-threatening. The pulse becomes thready in character, the skin pale and the level of consciousness depressed. Loss of 2.5 litres (50 per cent) results in loss of consciousness, and death follows soon after. So as Jesus was nailed to the cross, He was already severely physically compromised.

The means of crucifixion was such that the nails were almost certainly placed through the lowermost part of the forearm, not through the hands. The simple reason for this is that the body weight has to hang through these points, and the force involved is massive. Similarly the nails were probably placed through the ankle joints, rather than the feet. This would have given a solid anchor point, and also avoided the impossible situation of the feet being nailed to a flat vertical surface. The risk of penetration of the anterior tibial artery, running in this vicinity, would have been appreciable, resulting in further slow blood loss.

Returning to the massive force resulting from hanging a man by the arms, this can be calculated by a simple application of vectors. Calculation is inappropriate here, but readers proficient in physics can appreciate that hanging a 70kg man with arms outstretched at 85 degrees (i.e. just short of horizontal) results in a distracting force on each arm of almost half a metric ton. Within minutes the shoulders dislocate, with the elbows and wrists following. The effect on the torso would have been outward movement of the shoulder blades, to the extreme, with resulting outward stretching of the chest wall. Practically, this expands the chest cavity and makes the act of breathing very difficult. Every breath takes increasing effort, and can only be achieved by lifting the body on the impaled ankles. Consequently, Jesus would have been unable to maintain normal breathing patterns, and hence, control over carbon dioxide and oxygen levels. Specifically, respiratory failure occurs initially, with normal carbon dioxide levels, but slowly falling oxygen levels (known as a type I respiratory failure). The physical effects on the lungs are that fluid collects at their bases, compounding fluid loss and exacerbating the respiratory failure. After a while, therefore, the carbon dioxide level starts to rise (type II respiratory failure), and the blood becomes progressively more acidic (acidosis). This in itself damages cells and compounds the impending lethal effects of progressing from class III into class IV shock. Jesus would almost certainly have lapsed into and out of consciousness at this stage. The situation of profound shock and respiratory failure was constantly compounded by Jesus' vertical and static position. Death would have followed with inevitability, and appears to have taken six hours from the start of crucifixion.

John's Gospel records that when the soldiers found that He was dead, one of them pierced Jesus' side with a spear, bringing a sudden flow of 'blood and water' (John 19:34). This passage records that the legs of the still-alive robbers were broken to hasten death. They knew that this would slowly asphyxiate the victims, who had been relying on taking their weight regularly through their legs in order to exhale. This act of leg-breaking was therefore not only very painful, but a guaranteed way to watch slow death. The robbers would have become blue and gasping while the laughing soldiers mocked. If the victim was thought to be dead, the Roman soldiers were trained in spearing the heart to ensure death. The spear wound would most likely have penetrated the upper abdominal wall, the diaphragm and the lower thoracic cavity. This would have caused blood loss, which would have continued if Jesus were still alive. The fact that it stopped suggests that the heart was speared and its unclotted contents emptied, followed by fluid from the fairly sizeable collections at the lung bases. It is also possible that fluid poured from a ruptured stomach: enlargement of the stomach and stagnation of its contents are features of injury. It is important to note that the separate observation of fluid would not have occurred if bleeding were ongoing (i.e. if Jesus was alive). With such a spearing it is possible, though not certain, that a ruptured lung would have also occurred. The negative pressure surrounding the lungs inevitably means that one lung collapses. If inflicted on the left side, the spear may well have penetrated the stomach and then the heart. (History suggests it was the left side, though the Bible does not record this detail.) So, even if the heart were not penetrated, this major wound would have seriously injured the diaphragm and left lung. This injury alone, untreated, might result in death in an otherwise uninjured adult. This is especially so as a penetrating chest wound almost always causes a particular form of burst lung, which allows pressures to build up internally and compress the healthy remaining lung ('tension pneumothorax'). This also results in distortion of the major vessels, and is often a lethal injury.

Considering Jesus' appalling catalogue of injury, and for any who doubt that Jesus was dead, the effect of this would have been a dramatic compounding of the respiratory failure, acidosis, and a severe drop of the circulating volume below life-sustaining levels.

For all these reasons, the legislative culture of that period had good reasons to rely on crucifixion as a means of slow lethal punishment, guaranteed in its effects.

Historical evidence

The historians of the day provide ample evidence that Jesus was killed. The Jewish Talmud recorded that Jesus was hanged on the eve of Passover. Thallus and Phlegon, first-century historians, both documented the sun being darkened at the time of Jesus' death. An eclipse of the sun was given as the reason, though this could not be so as it was the season of the Paschal full moon when Christ died.

The three-hour period of darkness was noted worldwide, and was recorded in Rome by contemporary historians.

Cornelius Tacitus was a Roman historian, born 52–54 AD. He stated that Jesus had been put to death by Pontius Pilate. Flavius Josephus, born in 37 AD, was a Jewish Pharisee and wrote, 'Now there was about this time Jesus, a wise man, if it be lawful to call Him a man, for He was a doer of wonderful works ... Pilate ... condemned Him to the cross ... He appeared to them alive again on the third day.' (I have shortened this comment slightly so that it is easier to understand, without changing the meaning in any way.)

These independent accounts of Christianity never doubted the historicity of Jesus, which was disputed for the first time and on inadequate grounds by several authors at the end of the 18th, during the 19th, and at the beginning of the 20th centuries.

Further evidence for the resurrection
Besides the medical and non-Biblical historical evidence already covered, the Bible records that there were witnesses who saw Jesus alive. The New Testament records that 'after His suffering, He showed Himself to these men and gave many convincing proofs that He was alive. He appeared to them over a period of forty days and spoke about the kingdom of God' (Acts 1:3 NIV).

Paul wrote that 'He appeared to Peter, and then to the Twelve. After that, He appeared to more than five hundred of the brothers at the same time, most of whom are still living, though some have fallen asleep. Then He appeared to James, then to all the apostles, and last of all He appeared to me also, as to one abnormally born' (1 Corinthians 15:5–8).

Contemporary records such as these would have been torn apart if they had not been true. These words could not have been written without the people who were spoken of identifying themselves and agreeing.

If He didn't rise, then what happened?
Other alternatives to resurrection have often been put forward. Some have suggested that the disciples somehow stole the body and lied about the resurrection. However, there was a Roman guard, which was an ample challenge to a small group of fishermen. Most importantly, the authorities were obviously perplexed as to what had happened, and they themselves never seriously believed that the disciples stole the body. For example, no charges were ever brought, and no motive was ever established. On the contrary, from about this time onwards these disciples of Jesus became willing to die for their belief in the risen Christ.

Others have suggested that Jesus did not die, but merely revived after swooning on the cross. However, the evidence already presented indicates that this could not be the case, and Jesus' injuries were lethal. Even if they were not, how would He have escaped from a guarded, sealed tomb in such a desperately injured state?

Still others have suggested hallucination and hysteria on the part of the disciples. The fact that 500 were involved as witnesses to the sightings, as stated by a contemporary account, makes this unlikely. In addition, the fact that no one ever changed their stories despite widespread martyrdom makes this virtually impossible. An emotionally based belief, while sincerely held, would invariably lead to very inconsistent testimonies. The only remaining possibility is a miracle!

Specific details surrounding the crucifixion and resurrection were foretold

Actually most of Jesus' life was foretold, and space prevents a detailed appraisal of relevant prophecies. Just taking those prophecies relevant to the crucifixion and resurrection there are 13, mostly given 700–1000 years before Christ's birth. Their accuracy is astounding.

Prophecy: He was rejected.
Given: Isaiah 53:3 He was despised and rejected by men, a man of sorrows, and familiar with suffering. Like one from whom men hide their faces He was despised, and we esteemed Him not.
Fulfilled: John 1:10–11 He was in the world, and though the world was made through Him, the world did not recognize Him. He came to that which was His own, but His own did not receive Him.

Prophecy: He was betrayed by a friend.
Given: Psalm 41:9 Even my close friend, whom I trusted, he who shared My bread, has lifted up his heel against Me.
Fulfilled: Mark 14:10 Then Judas Iscariot, one of the Twelve, went to the chief priests to betray Jesus to them.

Prophecy: He was sold for 30 pieces of silver.
Given: Zechariah 11:12 I told them, 'If you think it best, give me my pay; but if not, keep it.' So they paid me thirty pieces of silver.
Fulfilled: Matthew 26:15 'What are you willing to give me if I hand Him over to you?' So they counted out for him thirty silver coins.

Prophecy: He was dumb before His accusers.
Given: Isaiah 53:7 He was oppressed and afflicted, yet He did not open His mouth; He was led like a lamb to the slaughter, and as a sheep before her shearers is silent, so He did not open His mouth.
Fulfilled: Matthew 27:12 When He was accused by the chief priests and the elders, He gave no answer.

Prophecy: His hands and feet were nailed.
Given: Psalm 22:16 'Dogs have surrounded Me; a band of evil men has encircled Me, they have pierced My hands and My feet.'
Fulfilled: John 19:18. Then were crucified Him and with Him two others — one on each side and Jesus in the middle.

Prophecy: His bones were not broken, but His joints were dislocated.
Given: Psalm 34:20 He protects all His bones, not one of them will be broken. Psalm 22:14 'I am poured out like water,

and all My bones are out of joint. My heart has turned to wax; it has melted away within Me.'

Fulfilled: John 19:33 But when they came to Jesus and found that He was already dead, they did not break His legs.

Prophecy: He was dehydrated and thirsty.

Given: Psalm 22:15 'My strength is dried up like a potsherd, and My tongue sticks to the roof of My mouth; you lay Me in the dust of death.'

Fulfilled: John 19:28 Later, knowing that all was now completed, and so that the Scripture would be fulfilled, Jesus said, 'I am thirsty.'

Prophecy: They cast lots for His clothing.

Given: Psalm 22:18 'They divide My garments among them and cast lots for My clothing.'

Fulfilled: John 19:23—24 When the soldiers crucified Jesus, they took His clothes, dividing them into four shares, one for each of them, with the undergarment remaining. This garment was seamless, woven in one piece from top to bottom. 'Let's not tear it,' they said to one another. 'Let's decide by lot who will get it.'

Prophecy: He was mocked.

Given: Psalm 22:7—8 'All who see Me mock Me; they hurl insults, shaking their heads. He trusts in the LORD; let the LORD rescue Him. Let Him deliver Him, since He delights in Him.'

Fulfilled: Matthew 27:39—40 Those who passed by hurled insults at Him, shaking their heads and saying, 'You who are going to destroy the temple and build it in three days, save Yourself! Come down from the cross, if You are the Son of God!'

Prophecy: His words before death.
Given: Psalm 22:1 'My God, My God, why have You forsaken Me?'
Fulfilled: Matthew 27:46 (NIV) About the ninth hour Jesus cried out in a loud voice, 'Eloi, Eloi, lama sabachthani?' – which means, 'My God, My God, why have You forsaken Me?'

Prophecy: There was darkness over the land.
Given: Amos 8:9 'In that day,' declares the Sovereign LORD, 'I will make the sun go down at noon and darken the Earth in broad daylight'.
Fulfilled: Matthew 27:45 From the sixth hour until the ninth hour darkness came over all the land.

Prophecy: He was buried in a rich man's tomb.
Given: Isaiah 53:9 He was assigned a grave with the wicked, and with the rich in His death, though He had done no violence, nor was any deceit in His mouth.
Fulfilled: Matthew 27:57—60 As evening approached, there came a rich man from Arimathea, named Joseph, who had himself become a disciple of Jesus. Going to Pilate, he asked for Jesus' body, and Pilate ordered that it be given to him. Joseph took the body, wrapped it in a clean linen cloth, and placed it in his own new tomb that he had cut out of the rock. He rolled a big stone in front of the entrance to the tomb and went away.

Prophecy: He would rise from the dead.
Given: Psalm 16:10 Because You will not abandon Me to the grave, nor will You let Your Holy One see decay.
Fulfilled: Acts 3:15 You killed the author of life, but God raised Him from the dead. We are witnesses of this.

The risen Christ can be known and He can change us

Jesus promised that it was important for Him to die, rise and go 'to sit at the right hand of the Father' because if He did the Holy Spirit would come. Indeed, about six weeks after the resurrection, the Holy Spirit came upon those who had believed. This was Pentecost, and its significance was far reaching.

Until that time, men and women had no realistic way to be changed. Although they could choose to obey God's instructions (His commandments and laws), this did not bring about any true change within. Suddenly, however, at Pentecost we could have the very Spirit of the living God within us. This brought the creative force that lies behind the entire universe into our hearts. Immediately at this point one might reasonably exclaim, 'Why are not all Christians transformed characters, therefore?' The fact is that this Spirit of God does take up residence within believers, but He is the Holy Spirit, and functions exclusively in the context of our obedience to His promptings. This point is easily lost sight of, and not as popularly taught as other aspects of the Spirit's work. Furthermore, His promptings are often costly to obey. So most believers find themselves in the school of obedience to the 'Resident Boss' (as Watchman Nee so aptly referred to the Holy Spirit). Our progress is sometimes painfully slow as we struggle with our wills. But the Spirit faithfully uses every opportunity to train us. Being one with the Father and Jesus the Son, He constantly offers us a closer walk with the Master, Jesus. And it is this walk which is so real, so sweet and so changing.

As a doctor I come across people who long to be different. One evening I was on duty and a 19-year-old girl, who had overdosed on a common painkiller, started to tell me about her life. Her boyfriend (and father to her three-year-old son) had introduced her to heroin, and regularly stole to get money for his own habit and hers. She felt trapped, and longed to rise above her captivity, but could not. She longed to be different, but the reality of life was already deeply ingrained in her, and she could not believe she could be any different.

Indeed true change is rare, a fact which frustrates those who seek to help some of the seriously dysfunctional people within society. This is why true accounts of how people's lives have changed are so powerful.

How medicine and faith in Christ are mutually supportive
Jesus spent years with fishermen, but never did He minimize the skill of fishing. But on the occasion when He said, 'Cast your nets,' great things happened! When He walked on water He wasn't trying to disprove any physical law. It is simply that the created world does not limit the Creator. Rather, He created it to function according to predefined norms, which we, as scientists, uncover. Initially it was so good. Before evil existed, all of creation was for benefit and blessing. But evil came and distorted love so that hate emerged. Evil turned benefit to damage, blessing to cursing. Energy was always intended for good, not for destructive bombs. Biological multiplication was always for growth and health, not bizarre viral infestation. Originally these norms were simply the physical definitions the Creator had placed His work into.

But at any time God can step outside these boundaries. And when He does, we see the most amazing of events. So we hear of laboratory confirmation of HIV positive patients with full-blown AIDS becoming symptom-free and HIV negative after simple prayer. We have authenticated accounts of terminally ill patients being cured, and patients with advanced pulmonary tuberculosis having no trace of their disease.

Such accounts cause some to say they are fake, or even the work of the enemy! But why should God not have the freedom to step outside established order if He chooses to? Jesus is the light of life, and all life flows from Him. He could not be contained in death, and He cannot be contained in the expectations we might have.

Let me summarize...

I believe in the resurrection of Jesus Christ because historical records that He lived convince me. The medical evidence that He died convinces me. All the details surrounding these events were accurately predicted, and I find these details convincing. The tomb was empty and I can find no tangible alternative to His resurrection.

The most convincing issue to me is that, being alive today, He changes people's lives. He heals people's bodies and minds. He is able to shine His light into our hearts and utterly transform us. And He is the light we will all see in due course.

31 WHAT DOES THE BIBLE SAY ABOUT HEAVEN AND HELL?

The Bible states that planet Earth is not the only place where men and women exist. Heaven and Hell are also very real places. So what does the Bible have to say about them? This chapter reveals all.

The authors hope that the reader is now convinced, beyond any possible doubt, that the Holy Bible is the unique, supernatural Word of God. Having arrived at that conclusion, we should all be very interested in what the Bible has to say about Heaven and Hell. The following is a brief summary.

Heaven

Few go there – Matthew 7:14
Created by God Himself – Genesis 1:1, Revelation 10:6
Everlasting – Psalm 89:29, 2 Corinthians 5:1
Cannot be measured – Jeremiah 31:37
Holy – Deuteronomy 26:15, Psalm 20:6, Isaiah 57:15
Where God dwells – 1 Kings 8:30, Matthew 6:9
Where God has His throne – Isaiah 66:1, Acts 7:49
God is the Lord of – Daniel 5:23, Matthew 11:25
God reigns here – Psalm 11:4, Psalm 135:6, Daniel 4:35
God fills this place – 1 Kings 8:27, Jeremiah 23:24

Where God answers His people from – 1 Chronicles 21:26, 2 Chronicles 7:14, Nehemiah 9:27, Psalm 20:6

Where God sends His judgements from – Genesis 19:24, 1 Samuel 2:10, Romans 1:18

Christ entered as a mediator – Acts 3:21, Hebrews 6:20, Hebrews 9:12, 24

Angels live there – Matthew 18:10, 24:36

Names of believers are written there – Luke 10:20, Hebrews 12:23

Place of joy when sinners repent – Luke 15:7

Place that the physical body cannot inherit – 1 Corinthians 15:50

Place of happiness – Revelation 7:16, 17

Kingdom of Christ and God – Ephesians 5:5

Father's house – John 14:2

Paradise – 2 Corinthians 12:2, 4

Wicked (unrepentant) are excluded – Galatians 5:21, Ephesians 5:5, Revelation 22:15

12 gates of pearl – Revelation 21:21

Streets of pure gold – Revelation 21:21

Glory of God gives light – Revelation 21:23

Hell

Many go there – Matthew 7:13

A place of torment – Luke 16:19–31 (probably the most vivid account)

Everlasting punishment – Matthew 25:46

Everlasting fire – Matthew 25:41

Furnace of fire – Matthew 13:41, 50

Lake of fire – Revelation 20:15

Fire and brimstone – Revelation 14:10

Unquenchable fire – Matthew 3:12

Devouring fire – Isaiah 33:14
Prepared for the Devil – Matthew 25:41
Devils are confined there until the judgement day – 2 Peter 2:4, Jude 6
Punishment there is eternal – Isaiah 33:14, Revelation 20:10, Revelation 14:11, Jude 7
Human power cannot prevent us going there – Ezekiel 32:27
Body suffers there – Matthew 5:29, 10:28
Soul suffers there – Matthew 10:28
Wise avoid it – Proverbs 15:24
Try to keep others from it – Proverbs 23:14, Jude 23
Associating with evil leads to it – Proverbs 5:5, 9:18
Devil and all his angels will be cast into it – Revelation 19:20, 20:10
Powers of Hell cannot stand against the Church – Matthew 16:18

32 WHAT DOES THE BIBLE SAY HAPPENS TO US AFTER WE DIE?

Some people sincerely believe that when they die they cease to exist – but the Bible states categorically that this is not the case. So what does happen to us when we die? This chapter attempts to interpret the Bible's answer to this vitally important question.

In this book we have recorded the accounts of a number of people who have had near-death experiences. The most important point made in this book is, however, the supernatural origin of scripture.

The following is an account of what happens to the human spirit after death, supported by both scripture and the testimonies in this book. By far the most reliable guide to life after death is scripture itself. The testimonies in this book can neither be proved nor disproved, but are simply interesting because they agree with scripture.

Millions of Christians down the ages have accepted the teaching of the Bible without access to detailed knowledge of near-death experiences. The authors of this book accept the Bible at face value, and would hold Biblical views irrespective of knowledge of any near-death experiences.

The human being is a spirit living in a body

It is interesting to study carefully the account of the creation of man in Genesis. We are informed that God is a Spirit (John 4:24) and that in the beginning God created the Heaven and the Earth (Genesis 1:1).

In the Bible, both in the books of John and Revelation, Jesus Christ is described as the Word. John's Gospel opens with the following verses: 'In the beginning was the Word and the Word was with God and the Word was God. He was in the beginning with God. All things were made through Him, and without Him nothing was made that was made' (John 1:1–3).

This clearly states that Jesus Christ existed as God before He was born as a baby in Bethlehem. He was present with both God the Father and God the Holy Spirit at the original creation.

The creation of the spirits of Adam and Eve

In many schools the Creation story is dismissed as a legend. However, Adam is described as the Son of God in the genealogy of Jesus Christ (Luke 3:38). Jesus said, 'From the beginning of the creation, God made them male and female' (Mark 10:6).

In Genesis 1:26 we are informed that God said, 'Let us make man in our image according to our likeness'. In verse 27 the text explains, 'So God created man in His own image; in the image of God He created him; male and female He created them.'

It therefore appears that God created the spirits of Adam and Eve, since God is a spirit, and created man in His exact likeness.

The creation of human beings

It is not until Genesis 2 that the actual creation of the human being appears: 'And the Lord God formed man of the dust of the ground, and breathed into his nostrils the breath of life; and man became a living being' (Genesis 2:7).

It is remarkable that the chemical components of the human body are exactly the same chemical elements as the dust of the ground. Our physical bodies are made up of about 17 chemical elements, the same 17 that are found in the dust of the ground (Chuck Missler, *The Physics of Immortality* and *From Here to Eternity*). It is a matter of common observation that, after a body has been cremated, only dust remains. If this dust from a crematorium were analysed we would find exactly the same chemical elements as the dust of the ground.

Thus it appears that the creation of the human body was a two-part process. First of all the spirits of Adam and Eve were created in the image of God, and then these spirits were breathed by God into a human body, formed of the dust of the ground.

To explain the above simply, it appears that the live human body is human flesh made of the same chemical elements as the dust of the ground, but with a human spirit living in it. Both were formed by God Himself.

At death the human body decomposes, but the spirit lives on. A spirit is indestructible. When one looks at a human being on this planet one is simply looking at the outward form, namely the physical body, which will one day die, containing an inner spirit which will live forever.

All human beings were created in the mind of God before the creation of the world

This is confirmed in Ephesians 1:4, 5: 'He chose us in Him before the foundation of the world, that we should be holy and without blame before Him in love, having predestined us to adoption as sons by Jesus Christ to Himself.'

The implications of this are very profound indeed. The Bible clearly states that each individual was chosen before the world was created. Both this statement, and the Genesis account of the creation of man, completely discount evolution. If the reader accepts the supernatural origin of scripture as explained in the previous chapter, there is no basis whatever for evolution in the teaching of the Bible.

When Jesus died His spirit left His body

The following are two scriptural depictions of the spirit leaving the body after the body dies.

'Jesus said "It is finished" and bowing His head, He gave up His Spirit' (John 19:30). According to the Bible, as Jesus' spirit left His body, He died.

A dead girl's spirit came back into her body, and she came back to life

Jesus was called to see a girl aged 12 who had died, with a request that He should bring the girl back to life again. The story is recorded in Luke 8:53–55: 'They ridiculed Him knowing that she was dead, but He put them all outside, took her by the hand and called saying, "Little girl, arise"; then her spirit returned, and she arose immediately.' The clear teaching here is that when the little girl's spirit re-entered her body, she came back to life.

After we die we are judged, and we will live in either Heaven or Hell

The Bible clearly teaches that 'Man is destined to die once, and after that to face judgement' (Hebrews 9:27). In the book of Revelation John records that

'I saw the dead, great and small, standing before the throne, and books were opened. And another book was opened, which is the book of life. The dead were judged according to what they had done as recorded in the books. The sea gave up the dead that were in it, and death and Hades gave up the dead that were in them, and each person was judged according to what he had done. Then death and Hades were thrown into the lake of fire. The lake of fire is the second death. If anyone's name was not found written in the book of life, he was thrown into the lake of fire' *(Revelation 20:12–15).*

Following the judgement we will live eternally in either Heaven or Hell.

Heaven

Scripture gives precise details on the nature of Heaven. The Bible speaks of the 12 gates of pearl in Revelation 21:21, indicating that the streets of the city are pure gold, like transparent glass. The Book of Revelation also speaks of a city of light with walls constructed of jasper. There are twelve foundations to the walls of the city, built of jasper, sapphire, chalcedony, emerald, sardonyx, sardius, chrysolite, beryl, topaz, chrysoprase, jacinth and amethyst, as described in Revelation 21:18–20.

33 HOW CAN WE MAKE SURE THAT WE GO TO HEAVEN, AND NOT TO HELL, WHEN WE DIE?

Since Heaven exists, surely it would make good sense to find out how to end up there – and not in Hell. The Bible has some specific advice on how to avoid Hell and be sure of going to Heaven. Read on, to find out how to spend eternity in Heaven.

According to the Bible an act of repentance and prayer is required. However, it is essential to be aware of some Biblical concepts before this prayer is prayed. These are explained below, with the prayer at the end.

Repentance

The Bible says we are all sinful. We need to stop being sinful, and ask forgiveness of God who is Holy, and will not tolerate sin in His presence. 'All have sinned and come short of the Glory of God' (Romans 3:23). 'If we say we have not sinned, we make Him a liar, and His word is not in us' (1 John 1:10). What in practical, simple terms does this mean to each one of us? Jesus said, 'out of the heart proceed evil thoughts, murders, adulteries, fornication, false witness, blasphemies' (Matthew 15:19). In simple terms this means obey the Ten Commandments. Stop murdering, adultery, sexual immorality, thieving, lying and swearing. We all have a conscience, which is God's voice within us (Romans 2:15). God will show each one of us what He does not approve of.

Who is Jesus Christ?

The Bible is perfectly clear that Jesus Christ is God. According to John 1, Jesus was there right at the beginning, at Creation, and He made everything. Life is in Him. To those who receive him, Jesus gives the right to become a child of God:

> In the beginning was the Word, and the Word was with God, and the Word was God. He was in the beginning with God. All things were made through Him, and without Him was not anything made that was made. In Him was life, and the life was the light of men. He was in the world, and the world was made through Him, and the world did not know Him. He came to His own, and His own did not receive Him. But as many as received Him, to them He gave the right to become children of God, to those who believed in His name. (John 1:1–4, 10–12)

Believe that Jesus is the Messiah, the Christ
The Bible is perfectly clear that Jesus Christ, and He alone, is the Messiah. We need to acknowledge this fact to God the Father, in prayer. Jesus clarified that He is the Messiah in the following text: 'The high priest asked Him, saying unto Him, "Are You the Christ, the Son of the Blessed?" Jesus said, "I am"' (Mark 14:61–62). According to the following text, we are liars if we deny this: 'Who is a liar but he who denies that Jesus is the Christ?' (1 John 2:22).

Belief in the Messiah will give us eternal life in Him, as stated in the following famous verse: 'God so loved the world that He gave His only begotten Son, that whoever believes on Him should not perish but have everlasting life' (John 3:16). A less famous, but very alarming, verse appears only 20 verses later: 'He who believes in the Son has life; and he who does not believe in the Son shall not see life, but the wrath of God abides on him' (John 3:36). To deny that Jesus is the Messiah invites the wrath of God.

Why did Jesus come to this planet 2000 years ago?
- To reveal Truth: 'I am the Way, the Truth and the Life. No one comes to the Father, except through Me' (John 14:6). 'He who has seen Me, has seen the Father' (John 14:9).
- To overcome Satan: 'For this purpose the Son of God was manifested, that He might destroy the works of the Devil' (1 John 3:8).
- To die for us: 'The Son of Man did not come to be served, but to serve, and to give His life as a ransom for many' (Mark 10:45).

Why was Jesus crucified?
The blood of Jesus, spilt at the crucifixion, is the blood sacrifice to atone for our personal sins. 'Behold the Lamb of God, Who takes away the sin of the world' (John 1:29). 'If we walk in the light, as He is in the light, we have fellowship with one another, and the blood of Jesus Christ His Son cleanses us from all sin' (1 John 1:7).

How then may I be forgiven of my sins?
- Forgive others: 'For if you forgive men their trespasses, your Heavenly Father will also forgive you. But if you do not forgive men their trespasses, neither will your Father forgive your trespasses' (Matthew 6:14–15).
- Forgive and love, especially your enemies: 'Love your enemies, bless those who curse you, do good to those who hate

you, and pray for those who spitefully use you and persecute you' (Matthew 5:44).

● Ask forgiveness from God the Father: 'If we confess our sins, He is faithful and just to forgive us our sins, and to cleanse us from all unrighteousness' (1 John 1:9).

What is a Christian?

A Christian is someone who has the Holy Spirit living in them. 'I will pray the Father, and He will give you another Helper that He may abide with you forever – the Spirit of truth, whom the world cannot receive, because it neither sees Him nor knows Him; but you know Him, for He dwells with you and will be in you' (John 14:16, 17). 'Your body is the temple of the Holy Spirit Who is in you, whom you have from God' (1 Corinthians 6:19).

It is not someone who tries to be good, attends church, reads the Bible, prays or does good to others, although all these are commendable. 'For by grace you have been saved, through faith, and that not of yourselves: It is the gift of God, not of works, lest anyone should boast' (Ephesians 2:8–9).

Who is the Holy Spirit?

The Holy Spirit is the Third Person of the Trinity. He is Holy, and He will not come and live in any of us until we are forgiven by God. The Holy Spirit is the creative power of the Trinity. It was the Holy Spirit who hovered over the waters in Creation, Genesis 1:2. As God said, 'Let there be light' (Genesis 1:3), it was the Holy Spirit who created the light.

Why must I be born again?

Because Jesus Christ, the Son of God, the Messiah, said so. 'Most assuredly, I say to you, unless one is born again, he cannot see the kingdom of God' (John 3:3). When we are truly reborn of the Holy Spirit, when we are 'born again' in the true Biblical sense, we become brand new spiritual creations. 'Therefore if anyone is in Christ he is a new creation. Old things have passed away. Behold, all things have become new' (2 Corinthians 5:17). It is, of course, the Holy Spirit, who makes us into a new spiritual creation. To be born again is to receive the Holy Spirit, God Himself, who comes to live in us.

If I am not born again, whose kingdom am I in?
We are all born into the kingdom of Satan, according to the Bible. 'Jesus said to them, "You are of your father, the Devil."' (John 8:44).

What happens to those who are not born again?
  The kingdom of Heaven is like a dragnet that was cast into the sea and gathered some of every kind, which, when it was full, they drew to shore; and they sat down and gathered the good into vessels, but threw the bad away. So it will be at the end of the age. The angels will come forth, separate the wicked from the just, and cast them into the furnace of fire. There will be wailing and gnashing of teeth. (Matthew 13:47–50).

   There was a certain rich man who was clothed in purple and fine linen, and fared sumptuously every day. But there was a certain beggar named Lazarus, full of sores, who was laid at his gate, desiring to be fed with the crumbs which fell from the rich man's table. Moreover the dogs came and licked his sores. So it was that the beggar died, and was carried by the angels to Abraham's bosom. The rich man died and was buried. and being in torments in Hades, he lifted up his eyes and saw Abraham afar off, and Lazarus in his bosom. (Luke 16:19–23)

The point is that the rich man closed his eyes and died in this existence, and immediately opened his eyes in Hell.

Jesus Christ is the only one who claimed to be God, has died, been to Hell, and been resurrected. He is the only one qualified to comment. He says that people who die without salvation, open their eyes in Hell.

What sort of prayer should I pray to be born again?

Jesus Christ loves you so much that He died for you, so that you could go to Heaven, and not to Hell, when you die. Shut your eyes and sincerely, and slowly, pray the following to God the Father, who loves you.

Loving Father, I want to be sure that, when I die, I do not go to Hell, but rather go to Heaven, to live with you forever. I need to be born again, as Jesus Christ, Your Son, taught us.

Please forgive me for all the sins I have ever committed, especially … (ask forgiveness for all those things highlighted by the Holy Spirit) … I forgive everyone who has sinned against me, especially … (name those whom the Holy Spirit shows you)

I turn away from all those things that I know to be wrong. Please show me all the other areas in my life that You wish me to change. Please forgive me because Jesus Christ, Your Son, died on the cross for me. I ask forgiveness because the Bible says that if I ask, I will be forgiven, because the blood of Jesus cleanses me from all of my sin. I thank You that I am now forgiven, according to the Bible, Your Holy Word.

Please now send the Holy Spirit to live in me. I receive the Holy Spirit. Thank You that I am born again of the Holy Spirit. Thank You that I have changed kingdoms from the kingdom of Satan, to the Kingdom of Jesus Christ, Your Son. Thank You that You are now my Father, I have been adopted into Your family, and that I have an eternal home in Heaven, with You. I commit the rest of my life to You.

Please speak to me about how You want me to spend the rest of my life. Please teach me about how I should live, and help me to understand the Bible. Please put me in touch with other genuine born-again Christians, so that I can experience true friendship with other believers, and be part of a Bible-believing church. Amen.

What should I do now I am born again?

- Join a church of Bible-believing Christians.
- Read the Bible. This is how God speaks to us.
- Pray regularly, asking God's guidance for all matters in your life.
- Seek to walk in righteousness.
- Have regular teaching.
- Seek to speak to others about the importance of becoming a Christian. 'Go therefore and make disciples of all nations, baptizing them in the name of the Father, and of the Son, and of the Holy Spirit' (Matthew 28:19).

34 WHERE WILL YOU SPEND FOREVER?

In the end, the real question is: 'Where will you spend eternity?'
This is one question that you can answer with certainty. No question demands more thought than this one.

The crucifixion of Jesus Christ is one of the most documented events in history, in both religious and secular books. We now live in the year 2000 AD, the Year of Our Lord 2000. Two criminals were crucified, one on each side of Jesus. The Bible says that we are all like criminals in the sight of God. The Bible clearly records the reactions of the two criminals to Jesus Christ, the Son of God, who was crucified between them:

> There were also two others, criminals, led with Him to be put to death. And when they had come to the place called Calvary, there they crucified Him, and the criminals, one on the right hand and the other on the left. Then one of the criminals who were hanged blasphemed Him, saying, 'If You are the Christ, save Yourself and us.'
>
> But the other, answering, rebuked him, saying, 'Do you not even fear God, seeing you are under the same condemnation? And we indeed justly, for we receive the due rewards of our deeds; but this Man has done nothing wrong.' Then he said to Jesus, 'Lord, remember me when

You come into Your kingdom.' And Jesus said to him, 'Assuredly, I say to you, today you will be with Me in Paradise.' (Luke 23:32, 33, 39–43)

Today one of the thieves is in Hell, and will always be there. He had an inappropriate reaction to Jesus Christ. The other thief is now in Heaven, and will be there forever. He looked at Jesus Christ, recognized that He was God, and that he, the thief, was sinful. The reaction of the second thief was quite different from that of the first. As a result he went to Heaven, while the first thief did not, and is now in Hell.

In this book we have presented the clear Biblical guidelines to becoming a true disciple of the Lord Jesus Christ, beginning with a genuine spiritual birth. It is the sincere desire of the authors of this book that the reaction of you, the reader, will be like that of the second thief.

This is why this book was written.

35 HAVE YOU HAD A NEAR-DEATH EXPERIENCE?

It is possible that, like the people in the previous chapters, you too have had a near-death experience. If that is the case, we would like to hear from you. This final chapter explains how we would like you to respond.

We wonder, what prompted you to start reading this book? Maybe you have read *The Final Frontier*, or one of the other Christian books dealing with near-death experiences. Perhaps someone you loved or respected has recently died, and you have started thinking about what happens after a person dies. Or maybe it was because you too have had a near-death experience, and were curious to know if other people's experiences were similar to your own.

One of us, David Waite, had a near-death experience, and for years never talked about it to anyone other than his close family. For a while David felt that it was too personal to share with the wider world, partly because it had given him a greater sense of God's love and care, and an excitement and anticipation of what he could expect the moment he dies. But gradually David began to realize that it was part of the package of experiences that God had allowed him to go through. He later thought that, at the right time and in the right setting, he would share his experience.

If you have had a near-death experience, or know of an interesting experience, perhaps you would like to share it with us, for inclusion in the next book, *Return to the Final Frontier*. Your story will not appear in the next book if you do not contact us! We can make your story anonymous if you prefer. We look forward to hearing from you. Thank you for reading right up to this page. May the Lord bless you on your journey with Him.

Dr Richard Kent and David Waite
Please write to us, or e-mail us at the following address, and we will promise to acknowledge your letter or e-mail:

Dr Richard Kent
Full Gospel Business Men's Fellowship International
UK Field Office
PO Box 11
Knutsford
Cheshire WA16 6QP
United Kingdom

Tel: 01565 632667
Fax: 01565 755639
E-mail: drrkent@aol.com

You may also like to look at the Final Frontier website at www.finalfrontier.org.uk, specially created by the Final Frontier Charitable Trust for this book and *The Final Frontier*.

When you contact us it would be very helpful if you would kindly include permission to publish your story in the next book, and also on the website. If you wish to remain anonymous, we can use only your first name, or change your name completely.

FURTHER INFORMATION

Choosing a church to belong to

There are many Bible believing Christians all over the world. Not all churches believe that the Bible is the supernatural word of God, so great care needs to be taken in choosing the right church. The authors are Bible believing Christians, and suggest that you join a Bible believing church.

Chuck Missler's teaching ministry

Chuck Missler's UK Address
Koinonia House
Calvary
344 Muir Street
Motherwell
ML1 1BN
Scotland

UK Tel: 01698 254848
UK Fax: 01698 336813

Chuck Missler's USA Address
Koinonia House,
P.O. Box D,
Coeur d'Alene
ID 83816-0347
USA

Tel: 001 208 773 6310
Website: www.khouse.org

Rev Chris Hill's teaching ministry

Rev Chris Hill
56 Holyrood Rd
New Barnet
Herts EN5 1DG

Website: www.clministries.org.uk

Christian Organisations

Full Gospel Business Men's Fellowship International, UK
UK Field Office
PO Box 11
Knutsford
Cheshire
WA16 6QP

Tel: 01565 632667
Fax: 01565 755639
Website: www.fgbmfi.org.uk
E-mail: fgbmfi@dial.pipex.com

Full Gospel Business Men's Fellowship International, USA
20 Corporate Park Dr, 3rd Floor
Irvine
CA 92606
USA

Tel: 001 949 260 0700
Fax: 001 949 260 0718
Website: www.fgbmfi.org

Helpful websites

Final Frontier website: www.finalfrontier.org.uk
Chuck Missler's website: www.khouse.org
Rev Chris Hill's website: www.clministries.org.uk
FGBMFI websites: www.fgbmfi.org.uk (UK website) and
   www.fgbmfi.org (US website)
New Christian Life ministries: www.newchristian.org
Christian testimonies: www.powertochange.com
Internet evangelism help guide:
   www.webauthors.org/guide/web-evangelism.html
On line magazine: www.soon.org.uk
Cartoon evangelistic tracts: www.chick.com
Biblical archaeology: www.wyattarchaeology.com

RECOMMENDED READING
AND LISTENING

Ankerberg, J. & Weldon, John, *The Facts on Life after Death* (Harvest House, 1992)

Baker, H.A., *Visions Beyond the Veil* (Whitaker House, 1973)

Bennett, Rita, *To Heaven and Back* (Zondervan Publishing House, 1997)

Blanchard, John, *Ultimate Questions* (Evangelical Press, 1991)

Buchanan, Alex, *Heaven and Hell* (Sovereign Word, 1995)

Chick, Jack, *This Was Your Life* (Cartoon evangelistic tract, Chick Publications, 1972)

Eastman, Mark, and Missler, Chuck, *The Creator Beyond Time and Space* (The Word for Today, 1996)

Eby, Richard, *Caught up into Paradise* (Bridge-Logos, 1989)

Fernando, Ajith, *Crucial Questions about Hell* (Kingsway, 1993)

Jastrow, Robert, *God and the Astronomers* (W.W. Norton & Co, 1992)

Jeans, Sir James, *The Mysterious Universe* (Macmillan, 1930)

Jeffrey, Grant, J. *Heaven: The Last Frontier* (Frontier Research, 1990)

Kent, Richard and Fotherby, Val, *The Final Frontier* (HarperCollins, 1997)

Lindsay, Gordon, *Death and Hereafter* (Christ for the Nations, 1986)

Maltz, Betty, *My Glimpse of Eternity* (Revell, 1996)

Missler, Chuck, (briefing packages) *The Creator Beyond Time and Space, The Grand Adventure, The ET Scenario, Beyond Coincidence, The Cosmic Codes, Footprints of the Messiah, The Physics of Immortality* and *From Here to Eternity* (Koinonia House, Motherwell, Scotland and Coeur d'Alene, USA.)

Missler, Chuck, *Cosmic Codes: Hidden Messages from the Edge of Eternity* (Koinonia House, 1999)

Morgan, Dr. Alison, *What Happens When We Die* (Kingsway, 1995)

Osteen, John, *Death and Beyond* (Lakewood, 1985)

Pawson, David, *The Road to Hell* (Hodder & Stoughton, 1993)

Pawson, David, *Resurrection* (Sovereign Word, 1993)

Payne, F.C., *The Seal of God in Creation and The Word* (Finck, 1979)

Pittman, Howard, *Placebo*

Rawlings, Dr. Maurice, *Beyond Death's Door* (Sheldon Press, 1979)

Rawlings, Dr. Maurice, *Before Death Comes* (Sheldon Press, 1980)

Rawlings, Dr. Maurice, *To Hell and Back* (Thomas Nelson, 1993)

Rees Larcombe, Jennifer, *Unexpected Healing* (Hodder & Stoughton, 1991)

Shapiro, Robert, *Origins: A Skeptics Guide to the Creation of Life on Earth*

Woodward, D. H. E., *Gems from the City* (Emerald Charitable Foundation, 1984)

The first book in this series: *The Final Frontier*

Dr Richard Kent and Val Fotherby

Warning – This book could change your afterlife.

Where do we go when we die? And is there really such a place as Hell?

Here are more than 20 stories from people who are convinced of the afterlife – because they've been there.

These 'near-death experiences' followed anything from heart attacks to car crashes and every person who tells their amazing tale is convinced they have seen what is beyond the final frontier of death.

Some tell of wonderful experiences of Heaven and the happiness they felt there. Others recall the spine-chilling moments when they realized they were in a place they are convinced was Hell...

Price: £5.99
Published by Marshall Pickering, an imprint of
HarperCollinsPublishers
ISBN: 0-551-03098-4

Ordering over the Internet
At the HarperCollins mail order website:
www.fireandwater.com

Ordering at any bookshop
The Final Frontier, ISBN 0-551-03098-4, by Dr Richard Kent and Val Fotherby